IMAGES
of America

THE NATIONAL ROAD
IN MARYLAND

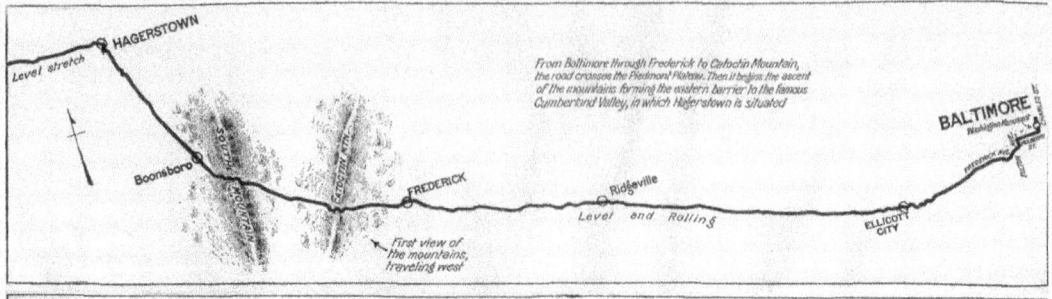
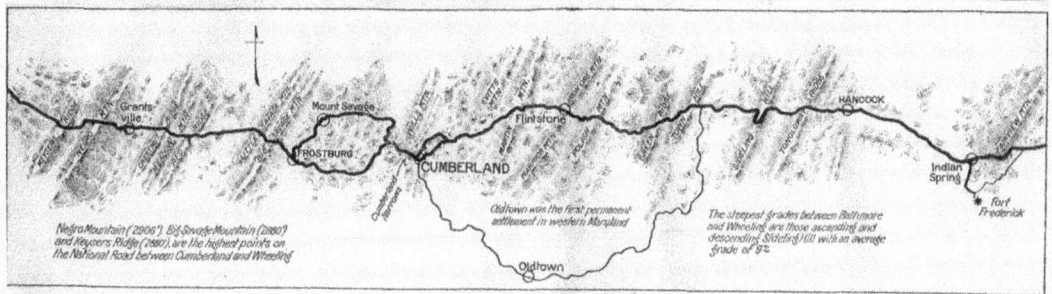

The original, federally funded National Road began in Cumberland and wound its way through western Maryland before crossing the Mason-Dixon Line into Pennsylvania. In the same time period, privately funded roads were constructed from Baltimore westward, eventually extending to Cumberland and linking to the National Road. The entire stretch of highway between Baltimore and the Pennsylvania boundary and beyond became, in common parlance, America's National Road. (Courtesy of Robert Bruce, *The National Road*, author's collection.)

ON THE COVER: For its first 15 years, the National Road labored over Wills Mountain as it began its journey from Cumberland westward. In 1833, the road was redirected along a circular route, which added several miles but was far easier than the original. The automobile in this photograph is entering a stretch of the later road after traveling through a deep valley known as the "Narrows." (Courtesy of Albert and Angela Feldstein.)

Images of America
The National Road in Maryland

Robert P. Savitt

Copyright © 2019 by Robert P. Savitt
ISBN 978-1-4671-0385-5

Published by Arcadia Publishing
Charleston, South Carolina

Printed in the United States of America

Library of Congress Control Number: 2019940810

For all general information, please contact Arcadia Publishing:
Telephone 843-853-2070
Fax 843-853-0044
E-mail sales@arcadiapublishing.com
For customer service and orders:
Toll-Free 1-888-313-2665

Visit us on the Internet at www.arcadiapublishing.com

For Michael and Jocko and their cohorts around the world: selfless companions who cheer and love us unconditionally as we travel the road of life

CONTENTS

Acknowledgments 6

Introduction 7

1. In the Beginning: A Bit of History 9
2. Mostly Lowlands: Baltimore to Frederick 23
3. The Initial Ascents: Frederick to Hagerstown 37
4. The Roller Coaster: Hagerstown to Cumberland 61
5. You Must Go Over, You Cannot Go Around: Cumberland to the Mason-Dixon Line 87

Acknowledgments

As always, my deepest gratitude goes to my wife, Babs, for her unconditional support and assistance in everything I do. In addition to her help in gathering images, she is my chief editor, proofreader, photographer, and jack-of-all-trades.

Books like this would not be possible if it were not for the gracious willingness of so many people who welcomed me into their homes, offices, and institutions. They generously shared their knowledge and advice and allowed me to reproduce the images that appear in this book. I am particularly indebted to Albert and Angela Feldstein for allowing me unbounded access to their extensive collection of Maryland and National Road–related images. This assistance kick-started the compilation of images and information on this history of the National Road.

Others who generously provided time and assistance include Jill Craig, George Messner, David Guiney, Tiffany Ahalt, Pam Williams, Mary Mannix, Carolyn Magura, John Frye, Elizabeth Howe, Marian Golden, Tracy Salvagno, David Wiles, Diane Kelly Weintraub, Ruann Newcomer George, Lisa Vicari, A. Thomas Fleming, Lorna Hainesworth, Shawn Gladden, Dan Materazzi, Paulette Lutz, Mike Eacho, Kim Bowers, Michael Johnson, Casey Pecoraro, Richard Weingroff, Doug Bast, John Seng, George Brigham, Julie and Ken Carbaugh, Winslow F. Burhans III, Jody Brumage, Yuri Zietz, and Jerry L. Harlowe.

Among the institutions that provided invaluable assistance were the Lewis J. Ort Library, Frostburg State University; Boonsboro Historical Society; Washington County (Maryland) Historical Society; Hancock Historical Society; Howard County Historical Society; Historical Society of Mount Airy; Western Maryland Historical Library; Clear Spring Historical Association; Middletown Valley Historical Society; Maryland Room, Frederick County Public Library; John Clinton Frye Western Maryland Room, Washington County Free Library; Maryland State Archives; Library of Congress; Enoch Pratt Free Library; Catonsville Room, Baltimore County Library; and the Maryland Historical Trust.

Introduction

In the year of America's 30th birthday, Lewis and Clark journeyed home after reaching the Pacific Ocean, Zebulon Pike failed to reach the summit of the mountain subsequently named after him, Noah Webster published his first dictionary, and Andrew Jackson killed a man who had accused his wife of bigamy. Oh . . . also in 1806, Thomas Jefferson signed legislation authorizing the construction of the young nation's first federally funded road.

The new road was to be the nation's first interstate highway. Along its route, it created and passed through the main streets of countless villages, towns, and cities. It raised thorny constitutional issues and spurred testy arguments at the highest levels of government. It stimulated trade and commerce, then took much of it away, and finally brought it back.

The new road has had many names through the years. Its birth name was the Cumberland Road, but it is most often referred to as the National Pike or the National Road. Other monikers include United States Road, Clay's Road, Hard Road, Baltimore–Cumberland Turnpike, Bank Road, US 40, US 40A, Maryland Route 144, and many others.

Why build a national highway? Albert Gallatin, the "Father of the National Road," explained that "good roads and canals will shorten the distances, facilitate commercial and personal intercourse, and unite, by a still more intimate community of interest, the most remote quarters of the United States."

In the years after the turn of the 19th century, the young republic experienced rapid westward expansion. Homesteaders were moving into the lands beyond the Ohio Valley. The territory acquired in the Louisiana Purchase beckoned other adventurers. There was a growing recognition that the mountainous barriers and long distances were threatening to create disunity in the fledgling nation. Where they existed, pathways across the mountains into the western territories were woefully inadequate to support regular travel between the regions.

In Maryland, trade and travel were constrained by the limits of waterways and the dearth of serviceable roads. There had been serious talk of constructing canals and roadways since the mid-1700s but no meaningful progress. Finally, in the first decade of the 1800s, charters were awarded for bank-financed companies to build toll roads between Baltimore and nearby towns. These were expanded to form a series of turnpikes extending to Boonsboro, Hagerstown, and Cumberland.

Simultaneously, support was growing in Washington for the federal government to finance westward road building. President Jefferson and many others were stymied by what were perceived as constitutional constraints on the right of the federal government to finance internal improvements within state boundaries. There was also the question of how to raise the money for such projects.

The debates over these questions were intense and complicated, as were the solutions. In essence, the state sovereignty question was resolved by requiring the consent of the states through which the road would pass. The fiscal issue was addressed through an agreement with the new state of Ohio to use a portion of the proceeds from the sale of federal lands in the state to help finance the building of the road.

It took five years of planning before construction of the Cumberland Road could begin. Ground was broken in Cumberland in 1811, and the roadway reached its end point, Wheeling, in 1818. The road was later extended to Vandalia, Illinois.

The road was an immediate success. A wide variety and volume of traffic traveled the new artery, and many commercial establishments sprang up to meet the growing demand for services. Existing municipalities along the pike flourished, and several new towns were created.

The golden age of the National Pike lasted until mid-century. The construction of the Baltimore & Ohio Railroad was completed to Wheeling in 1852. It soon became evident that road travel could not compete with the ease and superior carrying capacity of train lines. Almost simultaneous with the completion of the railroad to Wheeling, the Chesapeake & Ohio Canal opened between Georgetown and Cumberland. The canal did not have the impact of the railroad, but it did siphon some freight-hauling from the National Road.

The second half of the century saw a dramatic decline in traffic on the pike. Businesses floundered, and many ceased operations. The roadbed deteriorated dramatically. Writing of a trip along the National Road in 1879, William H. Rideing reported that "the national turnpike that led over the Alleghanies from the East to the West is a glory departed, and the traffic that once belonged to it now courses through other channels."

Soon after the article was published, the nation was hit with a bicycling craze. An advocacy group called the American Wheelmen began lobbying for drastic improvements to the country's roads so that bicyclists could enjoy a smoother, less hazardous experience. Around the turn of the 20th century, on the heels of this movement, America's love affair with the automobile began. The Good Roads Movement arose in the second decade, echoing the American Wheelmen's call for radical upgrading of the country's road system.

The combination of improved roads and affordable automobiles spurred a dramatic increase in tourism. The National Road became one of the most heavily traveled roads in the country. With this rebirth came the establishment of modern services: gas stations, restaurants, motor courts, and sightseeing attractions. Mechanized road building and maintenance equipment was markedly improved, leading to alignment adjustments along the pike. In the years following World War II, this led to wholesale construction of new road segments that bypassed the old National Pike in many places. The new roads became the "official" National Road or Highway in Maryland (now largely US 40, I-70, and I-68), and the old byways were redesignated US 40A, Scenic US 40, or Maryland 144.

Today, many intrepid explorers enjoy retracing the venerable road that carried so many travelers in Maryland from Baltimore to the Mason-Dixon Line. Two hundred years after its inception, the Old National Pike remains the "Main Street of America."

Note: Throughout this book, the terms *Cumberland Road*, *National Pike*, and *National Road* are used interchangeably.

One

IN THE BEGINNING
A BIT OF HISTORY

At the turn of the 19th century, the young United States of America had no shortage of obstacles in its efforts to maintain unity between the original 13 colonies and the western territories. Travel and trade were severely hindered by inadequate or nonexistent roads and by rivers that were difficult or impossible to navigate. At the same time, there was no shortage of ideas for solving these problems. Canals were deemed by many to be an excellent means of circumventing the waterway obstacles. Investors had formed companies and had actually broken ground. However, the planning, expense, and execution of these endeavors resulted in failure.

It seemed evident that the fastest way to encourage and facilitate travel was to improve existing roads and build new ones. There were, however, very few viable roads to improve and a lack of enthusiasm and capital to launch difficult and expensive new road-building projects, privately or by state governments. In the 1790s, several turnpike projects sprang up but not enough to successfully address the east-west divide.

In 1806, the stars aligned. Congress and the Jefferson administration agreed to fund and build a national artery from western Maryland to the Ohio River. While there were disagreements over constitutional prerogatives and regional interests, the creation of the Cumberland Road moved ahead, albeit at a slow pace. It took five years to finalize plans for the road and another seven to complete construction from Cumberland to Wheeling, Virginia. (The state of West Virginia was not established until 1863.)

Meanwhile, banking interests and private investors along the corridor between Cumberland and Baltimore realized the fiscal potential of a road stretching across the state and began constructing a series of "Bank Roads" to bridge the gap. In the 1820s, the roads came together, and a national interstate roadway was born.

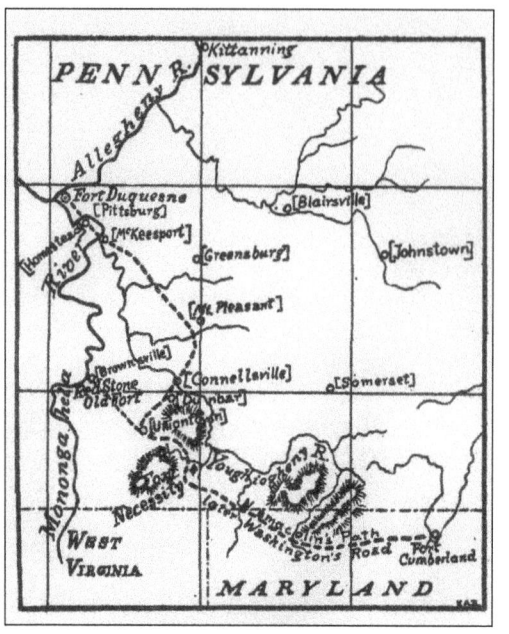

In the mid-1700s, the route from the central coastal colonies to the Ohio River followed a rough trail through the Cumberland Narrows. The path probably had been created by herds of wildlife and improved by Native Americans. In 1750, frontiersman Thomas Cresap and Namacolin, chief of the Delaware Nation, were hired by a land company to clear and widen the path through the mountains between present-day Cumberland and the future site of Brownsville, Pennsylvania (left). Three years later, George Washington was commissioned by the governor of Virginia to warn off French forces threatening to take control of the Ohio Valley. He hired Christopher Gist, a surveyor and mountaineer in western Maryland, to accompany and guide him on his mission (below). (Left, courtesy of Archer Hulbert, *Washington's Path*, author's collection; below, courtesy of *Emerson's Magazine* and *Putnam's Monthly*.)

George Washington's diplomatic mission to meet with the French in 1753 failed. The following year, Virginia lieutenant governor Robert Dinwiddie ordered Major Washington to lead a small force to assist in the construction of a British fort in present-day Cumberland. The movement of French forces in the Ohio Valley led to hostilities, which ended in the defeat of Washington's troops at hastily constructed Fort Necessity. The British sent Gen. Edward Braddock (right) and a strong military force to America to take on the French and their Indian allies. Braddock planned to travel from Alexandria, Virginia, to Fort Duquesne (present-day Pittsburgh) to confront the French forces. The old route along Nemacolin's Trail, however, was too narrow for the army's large equipment. Braddock ordered his engineers to clear and widen the trail to accommodate the army. The British expedition was ultimately defeated, but the improved artery was thereafter referred to as "Braddock's Road" (below). Fifty years later, parts of it helped shape the route of the Cumberland Road. (Right, courtesy of Library of Congress; below, courtesy of John Kennedy Lacock, *Braddock's Road*.)

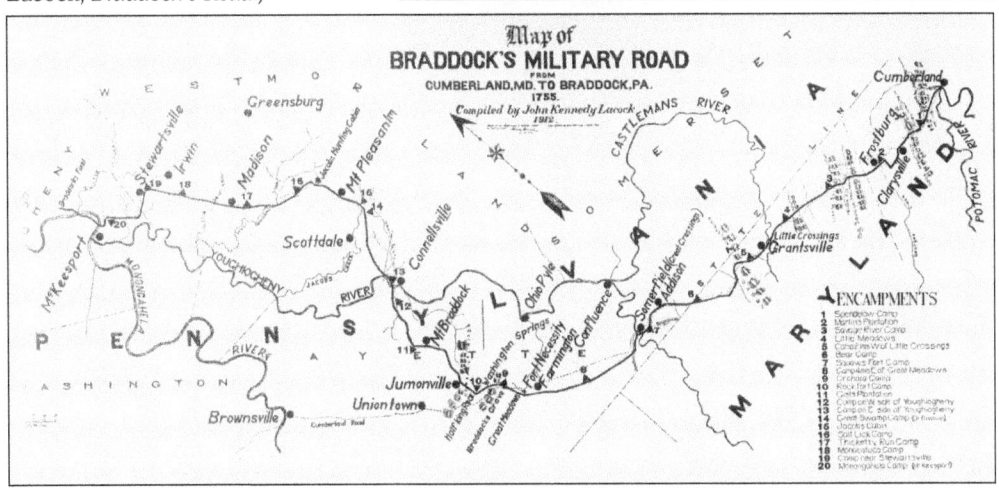

As the nation expanded during Thomas Jefferson's administration, it was clear that existing roads were inadequate to promote settlement of the new territories and trade with the original states. The chief proponent of internal improvements was Jefferson's secretary of the treasury, Albert Gallatin, shown above in conference with the president. Jefferson believed in a limited federal government but also recognized that natural barriers such as mountains would prevent the integration of the western frontier (e.g. Ohio and Louisiana Purchase territories) with the eastern states. The need for new interstate roads and improvement of existing arteries was complicated by a constitutional question: does the federal government have the right to fund internal improvements? If so, where would the money come from? In 1802, Gallatin promoted statehood for Ohio with provisions requiring that a portion of money raised by the sale of federal land in the new state go toward internal improvements. Four years later, Jefferson came to terms with the constitutional question and agreed to support federal funding of infrastructure. The image at left is the only know photograph of Albert Gallatin, taken by famed photographer Mathew Brady. (Above, courtesy of Federal Highway Administration; left, courtesy of Library of Congress.)

In 1806, President Jefferson signed "An Act to regulate the laying out and making a road from Cumberland in the State of Maryland to the State of Ohio" (right). The detailed legislation called for the appointment of three commissioners to travel to Cumberland, "view the ground" to the Ohio River, "lay out [a road] in such direction as they shall judge, under all circumstances the most proper," and prepare a report to the president with their recommendations. The commission's working team consisted of a surveyor, two chainmen, one marker, a vaneman, and a packhorse with a handler. In their initial report, the commissioners noted that "the duties imposed by the law became a work of greater magnitude, and a task much more arduous, than was conceived before entering upon it." Their final report was not issued until 1808. It is generally agreed that they did an admirable job and succeeded in meeting the requirements of the legislation. The head of the commission was Elie Williams (below), a Revolutionary War veteran who helped lay out the town of Williamsport and the Baltimore Turnpike. Williams later served as a surveyor on what became the Chesapeake & Ohio Canal. (Right, courtesy of Robert Bruce, *The National Road*, author's collection; below, courtesy of Washington County Free Library.)

When constructed, both sections of the National Road in Maryland (Bank Roads and Cumberland Road) were fitted with distance markers placed at one-mile intervals. Those on the old Bank Roads were made of local stone and, though varied in size, generally measured about 12 inches wide, 8 inches deep, and 30 inches high. The side facing the road displayed the distance from Baltimore. The mileposts on the federally funded road were originally made from stone but were replaced with cast-iron markers in the 1830s. They were painted white, placed on the north side of the road, and marked with the distance to Cumberland and Wheeling as well as intermediate points. (Courtesy of Babs Savitt.)

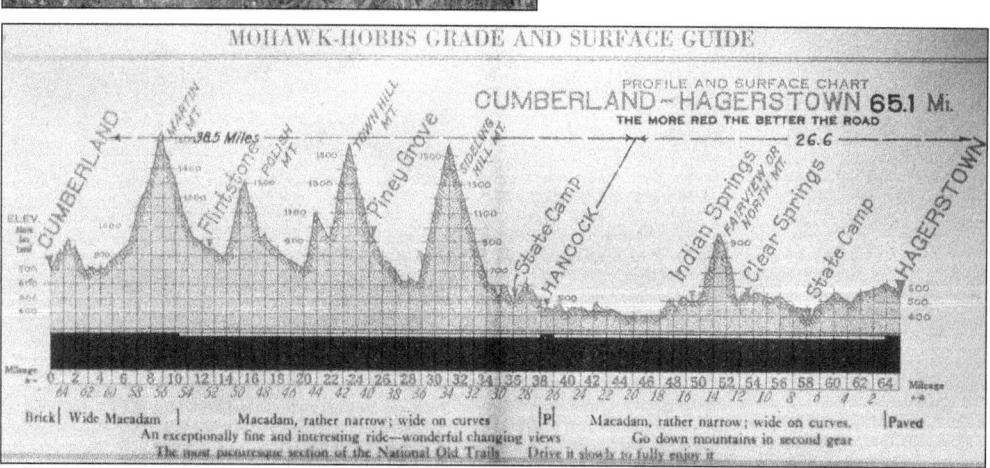

Mohawk-Hobbs Grade and Surface Guides were very popular with motorists in the 1920s. Published by the Mohawk Rubber Company of Akron, Ohio, the guides contained graphic depictions of the grades and surfaces of roads along with information on hotels, service stations, and sites of interest. The chart above covers the National Road from Hagerstown to Cumberland. (Courtesy of Albert and Angela Feldstein.)

Many prominent individuals traveled the National Road, including presidents, congressmen, senators, and leading personalities of the day. Among these was president-elect William Henry Harrison in 1841. As he traveled the National Road, he was met by crowds eager to see and hear him. In Frederick, he acknowledged in a speech that he was very weary. Nevertheless, the local newspaper reported that "his sprightliness in conversation" did not sustain "the reports of his senile weakness." Two months after his visit to Frederick, the new president died from what was reported to be pneumonia due to his exposure to the elements on Inauguration Day. Some argued, however, that he died "from the effects of a cold he had contracted while speaking in Frederick." (Courtesy of Library of Congress.)

Henry Clay was one of the strongest advocates of the Cumberland Road. His career included stints as Speaker of the House of Representatives, senator, secretary of state, and presidential candidate. Clay firmly believed that the federal government should play a role in planning and implementing internal improvements. His strong and sustained promotion of the maintenance and expansion of the nation's first federally funded road led some to dub him "Father of the National Pike." (Courtesy of Library of Congress.)

Stagecoaches were the aristocrats of the road. Their moniker was derived from their system of making stops at regular stages of the road. In his classic book *The Old Pike*, Thomas Searight recalled that "the coaches were all handsomely and artistically painted and ornamented, lined inside with soft silk plush." The three interior seats were "furnished with luxurious cushions" and could each "comfortably" seat three people. With a passenger seat next to the driver, these coaches could carry 10 travelers. There were other designs of stages plying the National Pike, with capacities ranging up to 12 or even 16 passengers. Some coaches carried mail or a combination of people and mail. Braking the coach was of concern to drivers and passengers. Writing of a trip on the National Road in 1840, William H. Wills explained that brakes "are pieces running across the bottom of the stage and by use of an iron crank which the driver uses, he can throw the break [sic] against the wheels and thereby impede their velocity." (Both, courtesy of Library of Congress.)

Conestoga wagons were a familiar sight along the National Road. Their primary purpose was to transport freight, but settlers often used them to carry household belongings and family members. These sturdy vehicles, drawn by four to six powerful horses, could carry enormous loads of freight and farm produce. The driver generally walked alongside the wagon or rode on the "wheel horse" (the left rear horse) or the "lazy board" (a plank that pulled out from under the front or rear of the wagon). Citing an article in a Philadelphia newspaper, Thomas Searight wrote that the name *Conestoga* was responsible for a popular nickname. Conestoga wagon drivers were known to favor cheap cigars. A Washington, Pennsylvania, manufacturer sought to profit from this hankering by producing inexpensive "roll-ups." They were originally called "Conestogas," but this was soon shortened to "stogies." (Both, courtesy of Library of Congress.)

In addition to stagecoaches and Conestoga wagons, a wide variety of farm and utility wagons frequented the pike. These were generally hand-built vehicles designed to carry small loads of agricultural produce or other goods. Not surprisingly, a wide variety of construction methods were employed in fashioning these wagons. (Courtesy of Hancock Historical Society.)

Aside from the extensive array of vehicles on the National Pike, herds of animals were frequent travelers. One young wagoner described the scene on the road during a trip in 1844: "[It] looked as if the whole earth was on the road; wagons, stages, horses, cattle, hogs, sheep, and turkeys without number." When tolls were instituted in the 1830s, herders were charged according to the type and quantity of their livestock. (Courtesy of *Harper's Monthly*, author's collection.)

Taverns and inns dotted the landscape during the palmy days of the National Road. It was not unusual to encounter one along each mile of the highway. In towns and cities, there were clusters of such hostelries. Most offered food, drink, and a place to rest or spend the night. Judging from most accounts, the down-home food was good, hardy, and plentiful. Homemade whiskey was inexpensive and varied in quality. Sleeping quarters generally were spots on the floor or shared beds. Some relatively upscale inns catered to stagecoach passengers, while others drew wagoners or other types of travelers. Many provided space for servicing animals or vehicles. (Courtesy of *Harper's Monthly*, author's collection.)

Inns and taverns faded away during the down years of the National Pike in the second half of the 1800s. With the coming of the automobile age in the 1900s, modern versions of the old hostelries began appearing. By the 1930s, the services available during the pike's heyday were well-replicated. Motor courts, cabins, restaurants, and service stations became staples of the highway, drawing large numbers of tourists and excursioners as well as commercial travelers. This establishment was near Cumberland. (Courtesy of Albert and Angela Feldstein.)

Most of the stone arch bridges constructed to accommodate heavy traffic along the pike proved highly durable. With some upgrading and steady maintenance, the bridges were able to withstand the influx of modern mechanized vehicles. In the years since its original construction, many portions of the National Road have been rerouted to improve safety and efficiency. Some of the original bridges remain in service, others have been abandoned and have deteriorated or disappeared, and some remain in limited service. Those still in existence have maintained the beauty that early observers commented on in many first-person accounts. The Savage River Bridge (above) was constructed sometime between 1815 and 1840 and, though removed from service when the pike was realigned, is still in limited service. The handsome design of bridges like this led to efforts by the State of Maryland in the 1900s to replicate the design in newly constructed concrete frame bridges. The structure below spans a creek on a realigned section of the National Road near Hagerstown. The Maryland Historical Trust reports that the decorative stone-like feature was added "to emulate the appearance and finish of the original nineteenth century stone-arch bridges of the National Pike." (Above, courtesy of Western Maryland Historical Library; below, courtesy of Babs Savitt.)

Construction began on the Chesapeake & Ohio Canal and the Baltimore & Ohio (B&O) Railroad on the same day in 1828. These projects made it clear that the days of the National Road's transportation prominence were numbered. It took 22 years to complete the canal from Georgetown to Cumberland. By that time, the railroad had been in operation for eight years. The effect on the National Road was disastrous. The greater speed and carrying capacity of trains resulted in a nearly complete shift of travelers and commercial goods to the B&O. With the exception of coal, lumber, and some farm products, the canal, too, was unable to compete. The National Road went into a nearly 50-year period of decline and deterioration. The canal operated until 1924 but never reached the success that its backers envisioned. (Above, courtesy of Library of Congress; below, courtesy of Western Maryland Historical Library.)

FARE REDUCED.
ON THE GREAT CENTRAL ROUTE via NATIONAL ROAD AND BALTIMORE & OHIO RAIL ROAD.

New Line of U. S. Mail Coaches,
For Washington City, Baltimore, Philadelphia, and New York.

THIS Line is in full operation, and leaves Pittsburgh daily at 7 o'clock, A. M., via Washington, Pa., and National Road to Cumberland, connecting there with Rail Road Cars to all the above places.— Travelers will find this a speedy and comfortable route, it being a separate and distinct Pittsburgh and Cumberland Line, facilities will be afforded which have not heretofore been enjoyed. Extra Coaches furnished at the shortest notice, with the privilege of going through direct, or taking one night's rest, at their option.

Fare from Pittsburgh to Baltimore, $10 00
Pittsburgh to Relay House, $10 00 ⎫
Thence to Washington City, 2 00 ⎭ 12 00
Pittsburgh to Philadelphia, 13 00

For THROUGH TICKETS, apply at our Offices, at Monongahela House, or corner of Exchange Hotel, and ☞ For seats in Washington, apply at D. Valentine's "National Hotel."

L. W. STOCKTON,
President of the N. Road Stage Co.
J. C. ACHESON, Sec'y.
March 25, 1843.—tf.

The coming of the Baltimore & Ohio Railroad to Cumberland in 1842 did not result in the National Road's immediate abdication to its rival. In fact, in the period after the railroad's arrival, the two modes of transportation complemented each other in some areas. The two notices pictured here offer travelers a combination of road and rail transportation to speed them to their destination. In the announcement at left, the National Road Stage Company offered to convey passengers from Pittsburgh to Cumberland in part along the National Road. They would then travel by train to Washington, Baltimore, Philadelphia, or New York. Passengers had the option of "taking one night's rest" or traveling all the way through to their destination. The itinerary in the notice below carried travelers by train to Cumberland, where they would transfer to a mail and passenger coach to Pittsburgh, Wheeling, or several other destinations. (Both, courtesy of David Wiles.)

GREAT UNITED STATES MAIL LINES,
TO THE SOUTH & WEST,
VIA
BATIMORE & OHIO R. R. TO CUMBERLAND,
AND
NATIONAL ROAD TO WHEELING.

SIX DAILY LINES of Mail and Passenger Coaches leave Cumberland every Evening, after the arrival of the Cars at that place, for Pittsburg, Wheeling, Cincinnati,

Louisville, St. Louis and New Orleans. Through to Pittsburg or Wheeling in forty-four hours. Passengers taking this route will be out one night only. Leaves Philadelphia twice daily, Winter and Summer. For Seats and Through Tickets, or entire Coaches, apply at the General Rail Road and Stage Office, No. 45 South Third Street, or at the Rail Road Office Eleventh and Market Streets. For Stage Companies,

T. BLACKWELL, Agent.

N. B. The above named Offices are the only Offices that are authorised to receipt through to Wheeling or to Pittsburg, via Baltimore. T. B.

Two

MOSTLY LOWLANDS
BALTIMORE TO FREDERICK

A traveler setting out in 1804 from Frederick Town to Baltimore with a large wagonful of flour would be facing 45 miles of rough, muddy roads and six long days of travel.

In 1792, the state legislature passed a bill authorizing the construction of a highway between Frederick and Baltimore. However, the heavy expense was daunting, and the project floundered.

At long last, in 1805, the legislature passed a bill authorizing a group of private investors to form a corporation to build the highway. The Baltimore and Frederick-Town Turnpike Company soon began constructing the road and setting up tollgates at regular intervals.

In ensuing years, Maryland experienced a rapid increase in turnpike construction. New corporations were formed, consisting of banks and private individuals seeking to promote commerce and possibly earn a profit through toll collection. While it soon became apparent that most of the funds collected were needed for road maintenance, the effect on commerce and travel was significant. The crowded roads greatly reduced travel time, but the increased traffic necessitated continual repairs on the deteriorating roads.

Nevertheless, road improvement projects continued, and the corridor between the busy port city of Baltimore and the thriving town of Frederick was soon to become an important link in a rapidly expanding highway system.

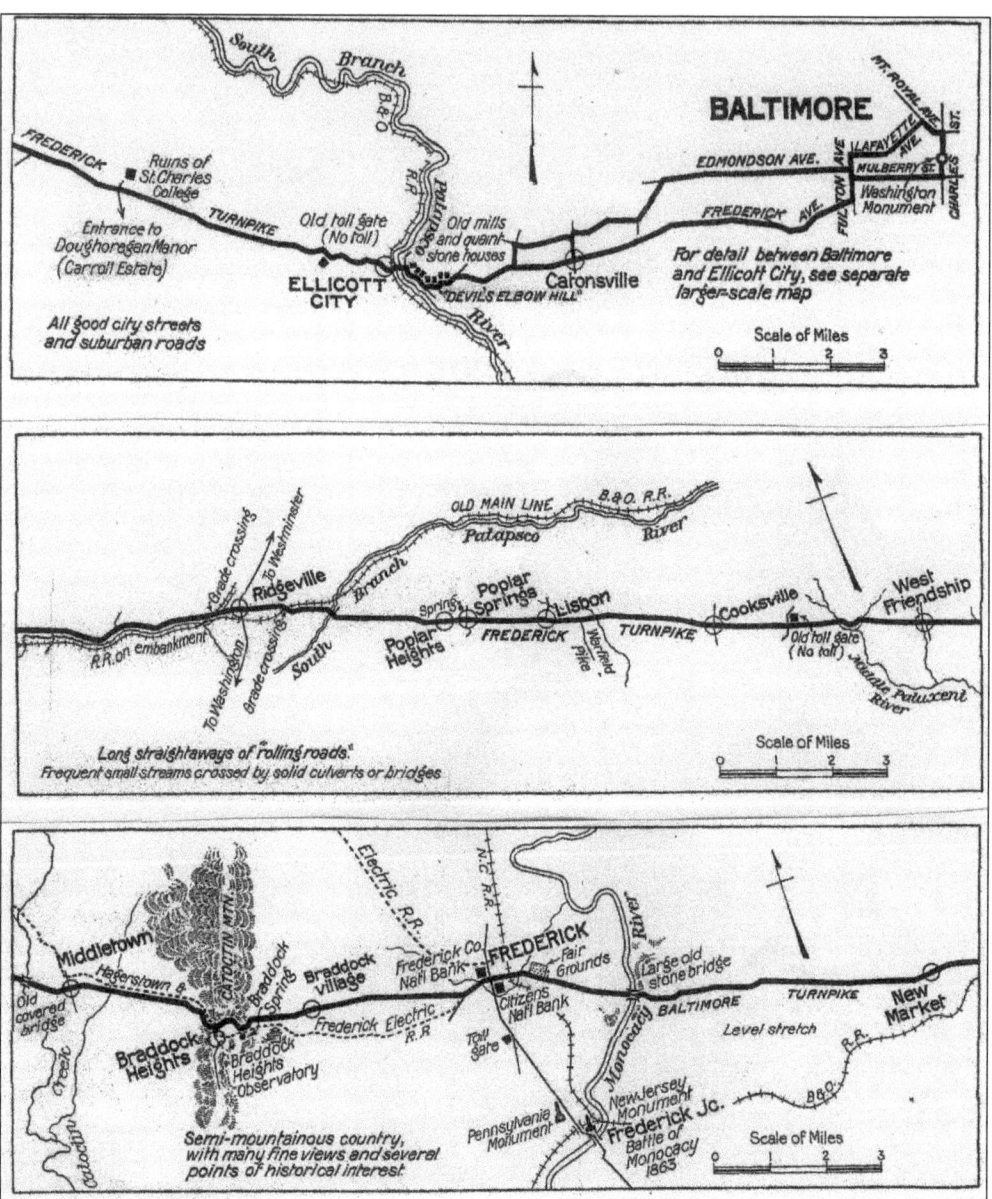

Most of the roadway from Baltimore to Frederick is relatively straight, climbing over small, rolling hills. In one brief section at Ridgeville (now part of Mount Airy), it ascends to almost 800 feet but quickly returns to low-lying, hilly terrain. The challenges of the National Road loomed ahead as travelers from Baltimore reached Frederick. (Courtesy of Robert Bruce, *The National Road*, author's collection.)

Travelers setting out from Baltimore on a journey westward along the National Road could choose from several routes out of the city. Using the original road link, a traveler would follow Baltimore Street (shown above around 1910) to Gilmor Street, Frederick Avenue, and finally, Frederick Road. In modern times, this route parallels US Route 40. (Courtesy of Library of Congress.)

Another route—often used by today's travelers—would follow Franklin Street west to Edmondson Avenue and ultimately to what is now identified as the Baltimore National Pike. In this c. 1900 photograph, carriages and people are making their way up Franklin Street. The old Calvert railroad station can be seen in the background. (Courtesy of the Maryland Department, Enoch Pratt Free Library/ Maryland's State Library Resource Center.)

In the early days of the republic, Philadelphia—served by a well-maintained road network—enjoyed a distinct advantage over Baltimore in commercial endeavors. The opening of privately funded roads linking Baltimore with the federally financed Cumberland Road in the early 1800s greatly boosted business activity in this port city. To serve the increasing traffic, taverns and inns popped up in the downtown area and at frequent intervals along the new roads. Older establishments such as the General Wayne Inn (left) benefitted from the growing activity. Constructed in 1785 and named after the storied Revolutionary War hero "Mad Anthony" Wayne, the inn was considered one of the more sophisticated hostelries in Baltimore. Its guests included Thomas Jefferson, John Quincy Adams, and Judge Samuel Chase. The Fairview Inn (below), another popular rest stop, was located on the road out of town. Its other name, the Three Mile House, pinpointed its location along the National Road. (Left, courtesy of *Scribner's Monthly*, author's collection; below, courtesy of the Maryland Department, Enoch Pratt Free Library/Maryland's State Library Resource Center.)

Until the early 1900s, Frederick Avenue was known as Old Frederick Road, harkening back to its origins as one of the arteries on the National Road leading out of Baltimore. Note the opening in the building across the road under the Bopp Brothers sign. The business started as a coal yard and expanded into a coal and lumber yard between 1910 and 1920. Apparently, judging by the sign on the building, Bopp Brothers also supplied ice to its patrons. (Courtesy of the Maryland Department, Enoch Pratt Free Library/Maryland's State Library Resource Center.)

The Frederick Avenue Bridge, built in 1930, carried traffic over Gwynn's Falls. The falls were named after the proprietor of a trading post and date back to 1669. Interestingly, there are no waterfalls in the area. It is believed that the term *falls* actually refers to the manner in which streams in the area topple over rocks, called "felles" by early settlers. The bridge was replaced in 2013. (Courtesy of the Maryland Department, Enoch Pratt Free Library/Maryland's State Library Resource Center.)

In the heyday of the new national highway, various types of animals, wagons, and stagecoaches would crowd the road in both directions. Beginning at the turn of the 20th century, horseless carriages became the prime means of transportation along the road. In this 1935 photograph, a "modern" traffic jam has cars backed up on the National Road outside Baltimore. (Courtesy of Western Maryland Room, Washington County Free Library.)

Seven miles west of Baltimore, the National Road becomes the main street of Catonsville. The town, first called Johnnycake after the delicious bread served by a local inn, was renamed Catonville after Richard Caton, a son-in-law of Charles Carroll of Carrollton, in the late 1700s. The "s" was added in the 1830s. The trolley line evident in this 1910 photograph was established in the 1890s to connect Catonsville with Baltimore. (Courtesy of Baltimore County Public Library, Catonsville Room.)

As the early turnpike was transformed into a portion of the National Road, Catonsville's main street—Frederick Road—grew into a busy thoroughfare dotted with commercial establishments that offered essential goods to residents and travelers. These 1898 photographs show the variety of provisions sold in two of Catonsville's popular stores along Frederick Road. The Old Corner Store (below), built in the 1830s, offered an eclectic mix of groceries, hardware, boots, and coal. The more exotically named Catonsville Accommodation Provision Store (above) occupied the bottom floor of a residence that probably housed the owner and his family. It is possible that among the patrons of these stores was John Wilkes Booth, a student for a year in the early 1850s at the Catonsville Military Academy. (Both, courtesy of Baltimore County Public Library, Catonsville Room.)

At an altitude some 500 feet higher than Baltimore, Catonsville attracted city dwellers seeking a cooler summer climate. The Oak Forest Park development was constructed on old property that changed hands several times before being divided into housing lots in the 1890s. This photograph from 1918 was taken at the entrance to the project. (Courtesy of Baltimore County Public Library, Catonsville Room.)

Steep climbs and spine-chilling curves were generally associated with the western portion of Maryland's National Road. The eastern segment, however, had its share of twists and turns. An area known as "Devil's Elbow" provided frightful moments to travelers between Catonsville and Ellicott City. In the above photograph, drivers are warned about a potentially hazardous curve as they cross a short highway bridge on the Frederick Road. (Courtesy of the Maryland Department, Enoch Pratt Free Library/Maryland's State Library Resource Center.)

In the late 1700s, three brothers purchased prime land used for growing grain and wheat on both sides of the Patapsco River near Baltimore. There they established a thriving milling operation and a community that ultimately grew to become Ellicott City. Along with the road (foreground), a train can be seen chugging along the upper reaches. The railroad, constructed in 1830 by the Baltimore & Ohio Company, was the first railroad line in the United States. It linked Ellicott's Mills with the port city of Baltimore. (Courtesy of the Maryland Department, Enoch Pratt Free Library/Maryland's State Library Resource Center.)

In 1787, long before the railroad came to town, the Ellicott brothers created a road to transport their flour to markets in Baltimore and beyond. When the Baltimore and Frederick-Town Turnpike was established in 1805, the Ellicott brothers' road became the first leg of the highway. The turnpike ultimately became a part of the National Road and ran through the main street of Ellicott City. As seen in this 1930s-era photograph, downtown continued to serve as a hub of travel and commerce. (Courtesy of Howard County Historical Society.)

The *Maryland State Gazette*, published in 1871, described Ellicott City as "undoubtedly one of the most romantic cities in the United States." The main section of the city, said the *Gazette*, "lies in a valley surrounded by hills, dotted with magnificent residences and beautiful churches." Evidence of this description can be seen in this 19th-century print. The town experienced a number of ups and downs in the ensuing years, including expanded industrial development, floods, downturns in its economy as plants closed down, and a resurgence in the latter part of the 20th century that has continued to contemporary times. (Courtesy of the Maryland Department, Enoch Pratt Free Library/Maryland's State Library Resource Center.)

Wagons of varying size and weight created ruts in the road and scattered surface materials. The herds of livestock traveling the highways added to the problem and produced roads in constant need of repair. The tollhouse (above) collected fees from vehicles and livestock owners as they trekked into or out of Ellicott City. (Courtesy of the Maryland Department, Enoch Pratt Free Library/Maryland's State Library Resource Center.)

As the National Road developed into a busy thoroughfare, the service industry kept pace. During the heyday of the road, travelers could count on encountering a tavern or inn every mile along the way. The Nine-Mile Inn (above), not surprisingly, was located nine miles from the highway's starting point in Baltimore. (Courtesy of Howard County Historical Society.)

The development of the National Road as an automobile route spawned a number of unique and memorable attractions. Many families traveling the road in the Baltimore metropolitan area as well as local residents were treated to a smaller and far less technical version of today's mega theme parks when they visited the Enchanted Forest. The park offered a fantasy world of amusements along with relatively tame rides. (Courtesy of Historic American Buildings Survey.)

The village of Lisbon was established in 1811. Bisected by the Baltimore and Frederick-Town Turnpike (later a part of the National Road), the town was a busy stopping point and thoroughfare during the prime years of the national highway. The Lisbon Hotel (above) grew up with the road. Over the years, it was transformed into the Drovers Inn, Poole's Country Store (with Millie Poole as proprietor), and the town post office. (Courtesy of Howard County Historical Society.)

At an altitude of 728 feet, tiny Poplar Grove was not exactly a mountain town. Yet it may have seemed so to residents of seafaring Baltimore. With its cool "mountain" breezes, Poplar Grove was a popular destination for well-to-do folks seeking respite from the city heat. Over time, the town was home to five hotels. The Poplar Springs Hotel (above) was a popular hostelry along the National Road. (Courtesy of A. Thomas Fleming.)

The National Road passed through Parrsville and Ridgeville in the southern portion of what is today Mount Airy. Ridgeville's elevation (830 feet) is the highest point between Baltimore and Braddock Heights on the National Road. Like Poplar Springs, its relatively lofty altitude and pleasant breezes attracted many vacationers and led to the establishment of a sanitarium for sick children. Parrsville was named after Parr's Spring, which eventually empties into Baltimore's harbor. The two towns have been absorbed into Mount Airy and no longer exist independently. (Courtesy of Historical Society of Frederick County.)

The original settlement in the Mount Airy area, Ridgeville, was established in the mid-1700s. A contemporary road from Baltimore passed through Ridgeville and ultimately became a part of the National Pike. The Eagle Hotel, originally called the Ridgeville Hotel, was built in 1877 along the pike in "downtown" Ridgeville. It was demolished in 1937. Today, a historical marker in the area includes the photograph above with this notation: "Located at the important crossroads of the National Road and old Route 27 (Mount Airy Main Street), the Eagle/Nelson/Ridgeville Hotel was a landmark for a century." (Courtesy of Historical Society of Frederick County.)

Historical geographer Charles Martin described New Market as "the consummate nineteenth century Road Town." Founded in 1788, the town grew up along an existing road between Baltimore and Frederick. When the road was improved and became a part of the National Road, traffic through New Market's Main Street increased dramatically and led to the establishment of numerous stores, taverns, inns, and wagon stands. One of the earliest post offices in the country was established in New Market in 1798. The building, like many structures in the town, remains standing today. The nominating form for the National Register of Historic Places notes that "the town has largely escaped the ravages of modern development." (Courtesy of Winslow F. Burhans III.)

One of the earliest inns in New Market was the Utz Hotel. Through the years, the building changed hands several times, serving as a tavern, general store, and most recently, a restaurant. The building stands today among many of the structures that dotted Main Street during the heyday of the National Road. (Courtesy of Vintage Restaurant.)

Three

The Initial Ascents
Frederick to Hagerstown

It is impossible to pass along the National Road between Frederick and Hagerstown without encountering stark reminders of the highway's key role in the Civil War. Although not in top-notch condition, the pike provided the most direct and accessible route for east–west travel in Maryland. Both armies utilized the road to reach sites where some of the most intense battles of the war were fought. The most notable of these occurred in the autumn of 1862, when Confederate forces occupying Frederick left the city and traveled west on the National Road toward Hagerstown. Union troops soon followed. The ensuing Battle of South Mountain was fought, in part, along the pike in the area where it crossed one of the mountain's gaps. This clash was followed by the bloodiest day of the Civil War—the Battle of Antietam.

In its prime, during more peaceful times, the pike carried an enormous amount of traffic between Frederick and Hagerstown, two of the largest towns in Maryland. Leaving Frederick heading west, the road gradually ascends 600 feet to Braddock Heights. The area saw little activity until the 1890s, when the founder of the newborn Frederick & Middletown Railway Company created a summer community at the top of Catoctin Mountain.

The road then descends into the Middletown Valley, where it becomes Main Street as it passes through Middletown. The author of an article in the November 1879 issue of *Harper's Monthly* opined that the valley was "as fair a prospect and as fertile and beautiful a reach of country as the world contains."

The road then climbs 1,200 feet to the peak of South Mountain before descending into Boonsboro. In 1823, the first macadam road built in the United States made the remainder of the journey to Hagerstown remarkably fluid.

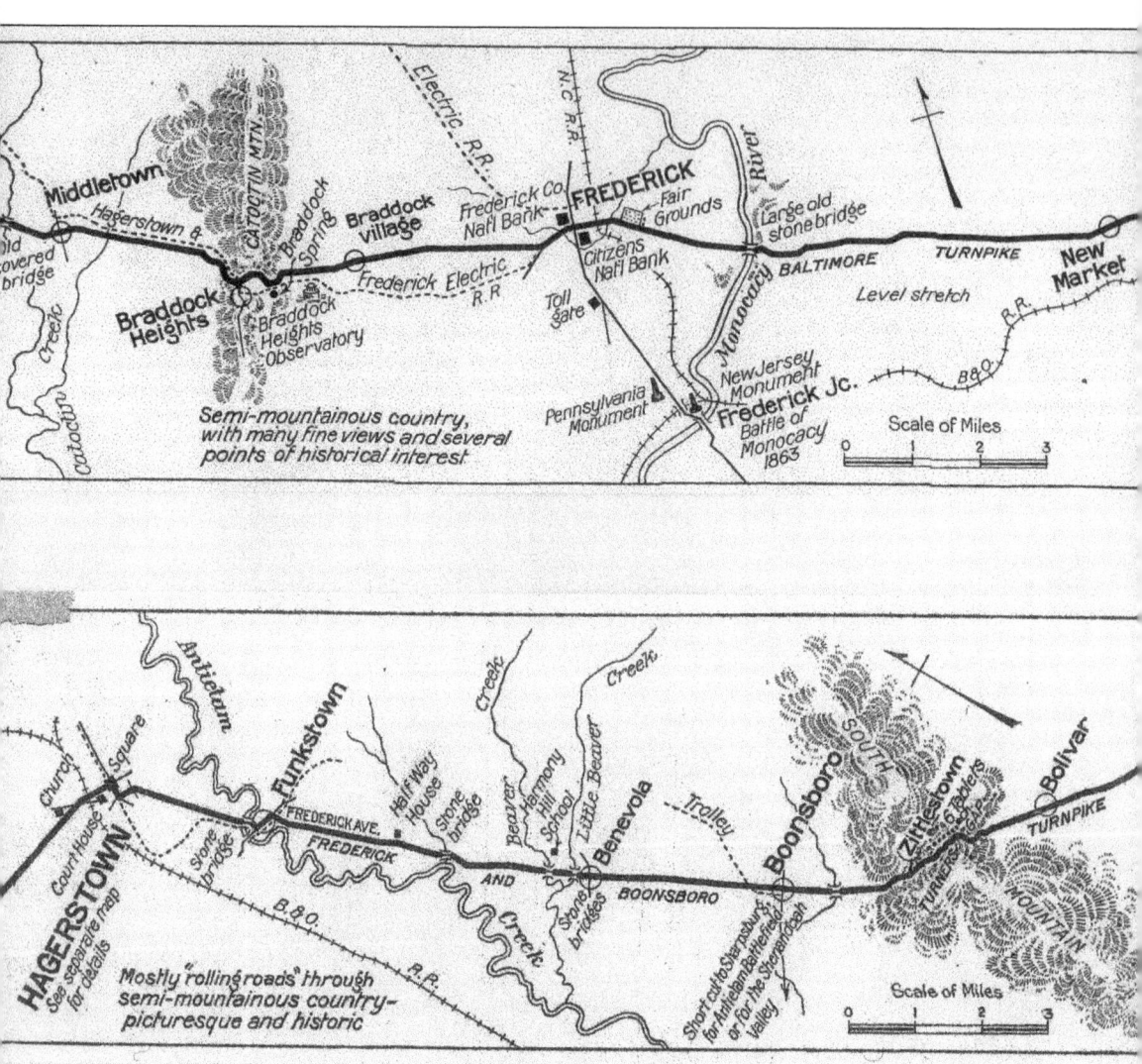

Braddock Village, originally named Fairview, marked the beginning of the climb up Catoctin Mountain to what became, in the late 1890s, Braddock Heights. This ascent to 1,200 feet, while difficult for horse-drawn vehicles, offered a preview of the steeper inclines ahead as the National Road traveled westward. (Courtesy of Robert Bruce, *The National Road*, author's collection.)

As travelers approached Frederick from the east, they came to a tollhouse (above) before crossing the Monocacy River. Ahead was the Jug Bridge, a well-known landmark along the pike. As can be surmised by the photograph below, the bridge got its name from the odd-shaped stone sculpture at its east end. According to the authors of a 1940 guidebook, the jug "is said to contain a demijohn of whiskey sealed up with loving care by the trowel master." In 1824, during the Marquis de Lafayette's grand tour, a delegation of Frederick citizens met the Revolutionary War hero and accompanied him to town. The 65-foot stone four-arch bridge was built in 1807 and carried traffic until 1942, when it suddenly collapsed. The jug survived and was moved to a nearby location, and a new bridge was built. The jug has been moved several times and continues to stand as a reminder of the venerable old bridge. (Above, courtesy of Historic American Buildings Survey; below, courtesy of Albert and Angela Feldstein.)

Frederick, founded in 1745, was an agricultural and commercial center for years before the construction of the Baltimore and Frederick-Town Turnpike. Upon entering the city, the pike becomes Patrick Street and meets with Market Street to form the hub of Frederick. It then continues west before making the first significant ascent in the eastern portion of the National Road. (Courtesy of Historical Society of Frederick County.)

A photographer taking this photograph in contemporary times would be standing in the middle of the intersection of Patrick and Court Streets, looking toward Market Street and the Square. On the left, instead of the New City Hotel, one would be gazing at the Francis Scott Key Hotel (converted into apartments). The Weinberg Theater would be on the right side of the street, across from the old hotel. (Courtesy of Historical Society of Frederick County.)

With the advent of the auto age, traffic on the National Road increased exponentially. This, in turn, spurred the need for automobile dealers, repair shops, and filling stations. The Ideal Garage Company, originally located on East Patrick Street (the National Road), met all three of these needs. The company began as the Ideal Electric and Machine Company in 1900 and continues in business today. (Courtesy of Maryland Room, Frederick County Public Library.)

The Old Stone Tavern was constructed several years before the National Pike was authorized but enjoyed an increase in business once the road beyond Frederick was completed. The tavern was strategically located at the corner of West Patrick Street and what is now Jefferson Street. (Jefferson was earlier called Telegraph Street). A Mr. Bowers, the builder and proprietor of the tavern, welcomed such prominent guests as Henry Clay, Andrew Jackson, and Daniel Webster to his establishment. The building was demolished in the 1920s. (Courtesy of Historical Society of Frederick County.)

The National Road acquired a unique landmark in 1863, after John Greenleaf Whittier published his famous poem "Barbara Fritchie" about a 95-year-old woman defiantly waving a US flag at Confederate troops from an upper window of her house. While many aspects of the incident have been credibly challenged, the house, story, and poem have retained their popularity through the years. The house, rebuilt after a flood in 1927, was a museum for many years and subsequently an Airbnb. (Courtesy of Library of Congress.)

Confederate troops moved through Frederick in 1862, prior to the Battle of Antietam, and in 1864, prior to the Battle of Monocacy. While there is no doubt that Confederate armies marched along Patrick Street (the National Road) during both campaigns, there are questions among historians about precisely where and when this photograph was taken—Patrick or Market Street and 1862 (Antietam) or 1864 (Monocacy). (Courtesy of Maryland Room, Frederick County Public Library.)

On July 24, 1868, Frederick was hit with a fierce storm that caused Carroll Creek to rise 8 to 10 feet and engulf the city. On Patrick Street (the National Road), the water rose five feet higher than previously known and caused massive damage. The Barbara Fritchie House was partially washed away. The photograph above, taken in the aftermath of the flood, looks west on West Patrick Street. The *Frederick Examiner* noted that readers could purchase a 5.5-by-7.5-inch copy of the image from the photographer's gallery. (Courtesy of Historical Society of Frederick County.)

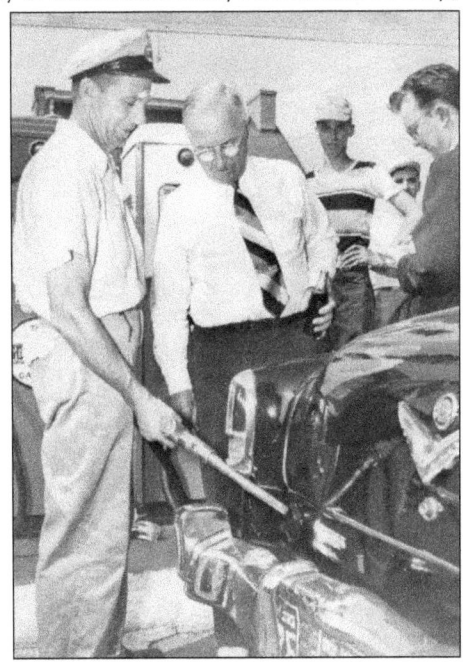

At about 4:00 p.m. on a peaceful Sunday in June 1953, former president Harry Truman drove along the National Pike into Frederick. He and his wife, Bess, were making their first trip back to Washington, DC, since he left office in January. President Truman pulled his 1953 Chrysler sedan into Carroll Kehne's service station on Patrick Street to fill up and imbibe a soft drink. The *Frederick News* reported that Truman had a Coke and his wife drank ice water. The president's daughter Margaret had alerted the media about his planned rest stop, and Truman was met by several reporters and photographers. (Courtesy of Historical Society of Frederick County.)

The City Hotel was one of the oldest and most distinguished hostelries in Frederick. It was originally owned and operated by Barbara Kimball, about whom a popular writer composed a celebratory poem. Joseph Talbott purchased the inn and changed the name to his own. Talbott's Hotel played host to many distinguished visitors, providing sumptuous formal dinners as well as refined lodging. In 1824, when General Lafayette was feted in Frederick, many of the events took place at Talbott's. The establishment was sold in 1831 and became the City Hotel. Following the Battles of South Mountain and Antietam, the hotel served as a hospital for wounded soldiers. The building was demolished in the 1920s and was replaced by the Francis Scott Key Hotel, which still stands along the National Road in the heart of Frederick. (Courtesy of the Historical Society of Frederick County.)

In 1755, British general Edward Braddock's army camped near a spring along the National Road on its ill-fated expedition to French-held Fort Duquesne. Braddock's troops constructed significant portions of what would later be associated with the National Road during this march. George Washington, who previously surveyed the route, served as Braddock's aide-de-camp. The stone in this photograph has a plaque affixed commemorating the journey. It has been moved several times and now sits atop nearby Catoctin Mountain. (Courtesy of Albert and Angela Feldstein.)

In his classic book *The Old Pike*, Thomas Searight wrote glowingly of the food at Hagan's Tavern in Old Braddock and reported that "the cheer within was exhilarating." The authors of a later guidebook described Hagan's as "a stagecoach stop where teamsters deemed it their right and privilege to celebrate with uproarious drinking bouts." The building (still standing) has housed bars, a speakeasy, an antique shop, and most recently, a restaurant. (Courtesy of Babs Savitt.)

In April 1927, members of the Federation of Rural Women's Clubs of Frederick County motored along the National Road to attend events in Braddock Heights and Middletown. The tour was part of a weeklong program to support the Better Homes project. The latter, endorsed by Presidents Coolidge and Hoover, aimed at overcoming the shortage of homes in the United States and encouraging thrift and efficiency for families. The group toured model rooms in Frederick homes in the morning, had lunch in Braddock Heights, and visited a home in Middletown. In the above photograph, it appears that the home in Braddock Heights is being deluged with luncheon guests after the attendees journeyed from Frederick. Had the women continued into Braddock Heights, they might have taken a turn on one of the park's most popular attractions, the slide near the Observatory (below)! The park was established in 1896 to take advantage of the accessibility afforded by the new trolley line and the National Road. (Both, courtesy of Maryland Room, Frederick County Public Library.)

The view of the Middletown Valley from the top of Catoctin Mountain captivated many journeyers along the National Road. Andrew Jackson, a frequent pike traveler, described the valley as "one of the most favored and delightful spots on earth." In this photograph, the National Pike descends into the Middletown Valley and is shadowed by the tracks of the Hagerstown & Frederick Electric Railway. (Courtesy of Maryland Room, Frederick County Public Library.)

With the arrival of the automobile age, speeds on the National Road increased exponentially over horse-drawn vehicles. However, moderation was the byword as cars approached towns. The folks in the above photograph were enjoying some hijinks, but the sign behind them was a serious warning to drivers approaching Middletown about the need to slow down. (Courtesy of McLuckie Collection, Maryland Room, Frederick County Public Library.)

The National Road doubled as the main street in most of the towns it passed through. As such, it was sometimes used for non-travel purposes. Parades, like this one along Middletown's Main Street, were commonly held to commemorate national holidays and celebrate local events. The marchers are traveling west and are passing one of Middletown's hallmark structures, the Zion Lutheran Church. (Courtesy of David Guiney.)

Snow could make travel along the National Road either more difficult or easier, especially for vehicles that could be equipped with runners. In this photograph of downtown Middletown in 1895, such a conveyance can be seen in the foreground as well as two other carriages parked across the street. Note the young boy in the center of the photograph using the National Road for sledding! (Courtesy of Rhoderick family.)

The National Road was a much-traveled thoroughfare during the Civil War. During their 1862 incursion into Maryland, Confederate forces under Gen. Robert E. Lee marched along the pike from Frederick through Middletown on their way to what became the Battles of South Mountain and Antietam. In this artist's sketch, the Union army is passing through Middletown's Main Street on September 13 on its way to the coming clash with Confederate troops. (Courtesy of David Guiney.)

While the National Pike was noted for its many handsome stone bridges, several covered bridges carried journeyers across rivers and creeks. The bridge pictured here was located one mile west of Middletown and passed over Catoctin Creek. It was burned by Confederate forces under Gen. Jubal Early in 1864 and rebuilt the same year. It finally met its end in 1923, when it was hit by a car, torn down, and replaced with a concrete crossing. (Courtesy of Middletown Valley Historical Society.)

The little village of Bolivar, located three miles west of Middletown, was established in the mid-1800s and named after Simon Bolivar, the liberator and national hero of several South American countries. It was one of 14 towns in the United States to take his name. At the height of its development during the years of heavy automobile traffic, the town boasted three general stores (including the Shank store, below), a post office, a band, and a baseball team. The post office was located in one of the general stores and was in operation from 1851 to 1901. As in many small towns, the general store welcomed local loafers who gathered regularly to relax with a mug of coffee, discuss and solve the problems of the day, and perhaps play some cards. The construction of nearby Route 40 after World War II and, later, Interstate 70 caused a significant drop in traffic and the dissolution of commercial establishments. (Above, courtesy of Maryland Room, Frederick County Public Library; below, courtesy of Jody Brumage.)

The gentlemen clustered on top of this coach appear to be on an excursion from Hagerstown and have reached the outskirts of Bolivar. The printing on the side of the vehicle says, "Hotel Hamilton," a large hostelry on Washington Street (National Pike) in downtown Hagerstown. (Courtesy of Washington County Historical Society.)

The Old South Mountain Inn is housed in one of the oldest buildings on the National Road. Built in the mid-1700s, the inn's storied history includes visits by statesmen, including Daniel Webster, Henry Clay, and several US presidents. In the first half of the 1800s, the building was a popular wagon stand, stagecoach stop, and eatery. During the Battle of South Mountain in 1862, Confederate general D.H. Hill used the inn as his headquarters. It became the private home of former Union admiral John A. Dahlgren's widow in 1876 and in 1925 became a tavern. In 1971, the inn was converted into its current role as a restaurant. (Courtesy of Babs Savitt.)

Another enduring hostelry was located only a few miles west of the South Mountain Inn. The Commercial Hotel in downtown Boonsboro was constructed in 1796 and was one of two stone buildings in Boonsboro. In its over-200-year life, it has been the Eagle Hotel, Chambers Hotel, Mountain Glen Hotel (above, 1887), Commercial Hotel (below, 1922), and Boone Hotel. One of its late-1800s advertisements promised "Good accommodation for man and beast at reasonable prices." An 1887 register, now at the Washington County Free Library's Western Maryland Room, lists guests from as far away as San Francisco and includes then-famous war correspondent and novelist George Alfred Townsend. The hotel's most recent owner is romance writer Nora Roberts. During a renovation in 2008, a fire seriously damaged the building. It was restored and today is called Inn BoonsBoro. (Above, courtesy of Boonsboro Historical Society; below, courtesy of Doug Bast.)

Boonsboro was settled in the 1770s by William and George Boone. In the early 1790s, the brothers laid out lots and established a town. The town was strategically located along the existing underdeveloped road created by Native Americans and early settlers and later by the ill-fated Braddock expedition. The new burg was named Margaretsville after George's wife. By 1805, it had become Boonsborough, and plans were in place to improve the existing road and link it with the forthcoming Cumberland Road. The town's name took on its present spelling in the mid-1800s. The above photograph of downtown Boonsboro was taken around 1900. (Courtesy of Washington County Historical Society.)

As "the Main Street of America," the National Road in downtown areas was bounded by shops and restaurants and was sometimes used for public events. In the photograph at right, Boonsboro citizens celebrate the end of World War I with a parade down Main Street. (Courtesy of Boonsboro Historical Society.)

The road between Boonsboro and Hagerstown was completed in 1823. It was the first artery in the United States to employ the new method of road building developed by Scotsman John Loudon McAdam. The process involved breaking stones into smaller sizes, layering them in the roadbed, and crushing them as vehicles traveled on the road. Careful attention was paid to water absorption, drainage, and other factors. As seen in the above painting, stone breaking was done by men arduously pounding with hammers. Note that (rear of image) horse-drawn rollers were used to compound the stones instead of relying on traffic volume. (Courtesy of David Guiney.)

The process of macadamizing and re-macadamizing the National Road continued to involve heavy rollers to compact the layers of stone. As can be seen in this photograph, the development of the combustion engine led to the replacement of horse-drawn rollers with machine-driven equipment. (Courtesy of David Guiney.)

In 1888, William F. Bast began work as an apprentice to cabinetmaker John Brining. Like most such furniture makers of the time, the business included casket making and funeral direction. Bast eventually partnered with Brining and then bought him out to start his own business. The company later separated the furniture and funeral enterprises and occupied separate buildings. The original Brining-Bast sign resides now with William Bast's grandson Doug, who established a unique, artifact-packed museum in Boonsboro. (Courtesy of Doug Bast and Boonsboro Historical Society.)

The tiny hamlet of Benevola was established in the 1790s with the construction of a gristmill. The routing of the Boonsboro–Hagerstown Turnpike through the community and the link-up with the National Pike provided a ready means of getting produce and goods to markets in Hagerstown, Frederick, and Baltimore. Though the community was never more than a small farming and milling center, it eventually sprouted a store, post office, houses, and several mills. Benevola was also the site of one of the pike's toll booths. The drawing above provides a view of the village's "downtown" area in 1847. Kline's Mill (below) on the National Road was a community institution. It was established in 1900 as the Benevola Roller Mill and made cider and apple butter as well as flour and other products. In later years, its Kline's Blue Ribbon Flour became a local favorite. (Both, courtesy of Ruann Newcomer George.)

The local hangout in Benevola as well as a fixture on the pike was the village store. The building was constructed in 1831, and in addition to selling a little bit of everything, it served as the community's post office when local postal service began in 1850. The person in the photograph is J. William "Pop" Stine, the store's proprietor from 1928 to 1952. (Courtesy of Ruann Newcomer George.)

Benevola is Latin for "well-wishing." In a 2004 interview in a local magazine, one lifelong resident anecdotally supported this sentiment. Recalling a fifth-grade assignment to list the attributes of the town his ancestors pioneered, the interviewee wrote: "1. Kline's Mill, 2. the State Road (National Pike), 3. the Large [community] church, 4. clean yards, 5. the school, 6. kind people." Spiritual life revolved around the Benevola United Brethren in Christ Church. Sitting just off the National Road, the church was founded in 1848. Its original building was constructed 10 years later. It was torn down in 1886 and a new church built on the site. (Courtesy of Benevola United Methodist Church.)

Funkstown was established in 1767 by Jacob Funck, who named it Jerusalem. Early settlers referred to it as "Funck's Jerusalem Town." The village was set on an early wagon road, which was modernized to become a turnpike in the early 1800s. Several years later, the road was incorporated into the Boonsboro–Hagerstown Turnpike. When completed in 1823, it represented the final link in the road chain between Baltimore and Hagerstown and a de facto part of the expanding National Road. Its central artery, Baltimore Street, became another main street along the pike. In this photograph, taken in 1914, the workmen are repaving Baltimore Street. (Courtesy of Western Maryland Room, Washington County Free Library.)

In 1769, Jacob Funck moved his family into a stone home constructed for him in his newly established Jerusalem Town. The home is still standing and is among the oldest structures in Funkstown. It is believed to have become South's Inn in the 1800s and has been cited as a stopping point for John Brown in June 1859, when he was transporting arms and supplies for his forthcoming raid on Harpers Ferry. (Courtesy of Babs Savitt.)

This beautiful three-arch stone bridge was constructed in 1823 to carry the National Road over Antietam Creek. The stress of heavy traffic led to a controversial widening and alteration of the bridge in 1931. In the words of photographer-reporter David T. Cottingham, the bridge "was irreparably mutilated, aesthetically." While Funkstown's military history is generally connected to events during the Civil War, the first "Battle of Funkstown" was fought between local citizens on this bridge while it was still being constructed. Irish workmen clashed with local factory workers who had been severely taunting them. Local militia forces were called out to quell the disturbance. (Courtesy of Maryland State Highway Administration.)

The National Road was extensively used and crossed many times during the Civil War. In 1862, the Confederate army passed through Funkstown on its way north and again on its way back for the Battle of Antietam. During the Confederate retreat after the Battle of Gettysburg in July 1863, Confederate forces under Gen. J.E.B. Stuart clashed in Funkstown with Union forces pursuing Lee's army. (Courtesy of Western Maryland Room, Washington County Free Library.)

Funds for maintenance of the bank-financed portion of the National Road (Baltimore to Cumberland) were raised through the collection of tolls. The fee was based on the type of conveyance or livestock passing along the road. Toll keepers generally lived with their families in small homes built alongside the gated road. While not arduous, the job required a willingness to be aroused at all hours of the night as well as at more normal daytime hours. Many tollgate operators supplemented their incomes through activities that could be performed in or near the tollhouse. (Courtesy of Washington County Historical Society.)

Hagerstown was undoubtedly a welcome site to weary journeyers. The city was home to some of the best-known inns and taverns along the pike. One, the Globe Inn, could truthfully boast that "Washington slept here." It stood on the site of today's University System of Hagerstown. Farther to the west stood the popular Buck Tavern (left), named for the portrait of a large buck on its swinging entrance door. The enclosure at the rear of the building was the scene of the cruel but popular "sport" of cockfighting. (Courtesy of Washington County Historical Society.)

Four

THE ROLLER COASTER

HAGERSTOWN TO CUMBERLAND

In his 1879 *Harper's Monthly* travelogue, William H. Rideing provided a curmudgeonly view of the National Road's steep decline. For the most part, Rideing wrote of sleepy backward towns, indigent people, and quirky experiences. The one aspect of the Maryland portion of the pike that he could not fault were the incredible vistas. The road between Clear Spring and Hancock "approaches in beauty the grandest passes of the Sierras." The ride down Sideling Hill runs "through avenues of pines and over rushing little brooklets, spreading their crystal force across the road."

One hundred and twenty years later, geographer Charles J. Farmer echoed Rideing's acclaim of the captivating terrain but complained of some of the modernized appurtenances along the road. A large convenience store, he wrote, with its "bold red, yellow, and orange colors," is "a color explosion . . . [that] stretches one's aesthetic tolerance to the limit." The beautiful Wilson Bridge, built in 1819, was threatened with demolition in 1983 before being rescued by preservationists.

This segment of road between Hagerstown and Cumberland owes its magnetic beauty to its stark, undulating mountain peaks and valleys. The rise and drop on Sideling Hill were the longest on the old pike between Baltimore and Wheeling, West Virginia. Robert Bruce, writing of a trip in 1914, reported that the road ascended 760 feet in one and a half miles and descended 495 feet in one mile. It ended with a challenging horseshoe curve. The many twists and turns on the road were challenging but manageable, although "one should not stop on the curves to view the scenery."

The peaks on this segment, though not equal to the many higher mountains in other regions of the country, presented breathtaking, multistate views. The surrounding terrain varied from thick forests to lush fields. In Robert Bruce's words, the vistas beheld by motorists were "beautiful beyond anticipation."

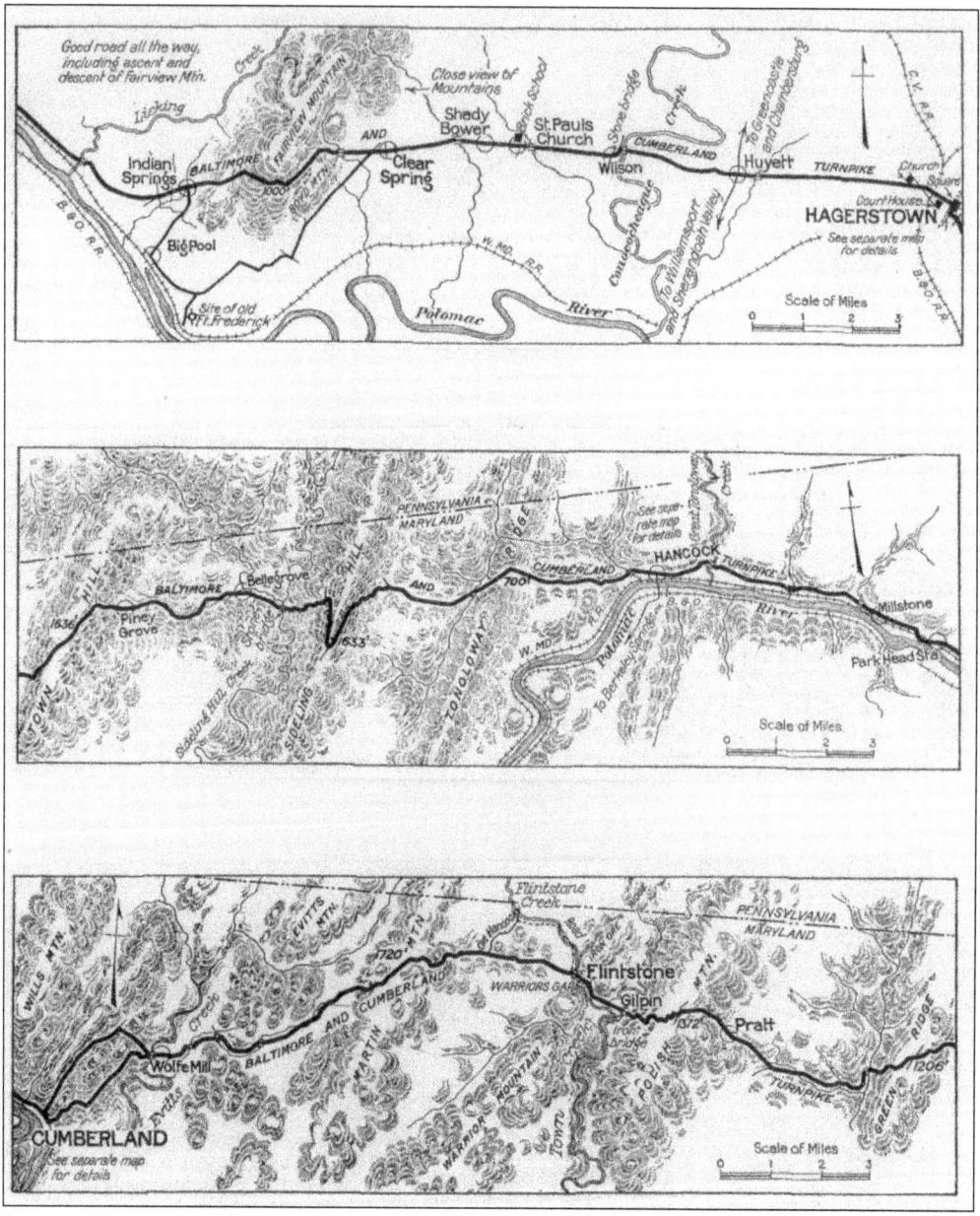

Leaving Hagerstown, the National Road climbs Fairview Mountain (1,000 feet) and then heads to the Potomac River near Hancock. Soon after departing Hanover, the roadway begins its unrelenting curves, hairpin turns, and challenging climbs. With their unreliable braking systems, horse-drawn vehicles often faced hazardous descents. (Courtesy of Robert Bruce, *The National Road*, author's collection.)

Author Robert Bruce described Hagerstown in 1916 as "an interesting old city in Central Maryland." Jonathan Hager settled in the area in 1737 and established the town in 1762. Originally named Elizabeth Town after Hager's wife, the growing settlement was renamed Hager's Town in 1814. It earned its moniker—"the Hub City"—as myriad roads, spearheaded by the National Pike, made it the crossroads of the region. It continued as a transportation hub when railroads were developed and, in the automobile age, maintained that role through an extensive road network running into and out of the city. The National Road travels for a short distance along South Potomac Street before turning onto Washington Street. The photograph above was taken from the Public Square at the point where South Potomac Street ends and the National Road turns right. (Courtesy of Western Maryland Historical Library.)

The original National Road ran to Hagerstown's Public Square, the heart of the city. It then made a sharp turn and headed west out of the city. The square began to form its character by the late 1700s, when the city was beginning to grow rapidly. The county courthouse and the town market, constructed in the late 1700s, were located on the square. The market's location made it easily accessible to farmers and consumers. The market subsequently moved to the basement of the courthouse, where space was created for carts and wagons to easily pull up. The city's growth and the need to relieve traffic congestion eventually led to both entities moving. The square, however, remained the center of business activity. In the above photograph, probably taken in the late 1890s, the open-air trolley and attire of the cart driver indicate that it is summer. The image below is from 1905 and shows three enclosed trolleys. The vehicles on the left and at center are leaving Washington Street (the National Road) and entering the square. (Both, courtesy of the Western Maryland Historical Library.)

After reaching the Public Square heading west, the National Road carried traffic along one of Hagerstown's busiest streets. Some of the city's oldest structures, many of which date to the halcyon years of the pike, line West Washington Street. Despite the street's importance, it was not always kept in the best of shape. The photograph at right, taken in 1880, shows a muddy and somewhat torn up West Washington Street. (Courtesy of David Wiles.)

Three modes of transportation are visible in this late-1890s photograph. The popularity of bicycles (between the two carts) was at its peak during this period. Trolleys (note the tracks) began operating in Hagerstown in the mid-1890s. Horse-drawn carts were still the preferred means of transportation, since the horseless buggy was still in its infancy. (Courtesy of David Wiles.)

The Blue Ridge Hotel, located along the route of the National Pike on West Washington Street, was constructed in the 1860s as the Hoover House. When the Hoover family sold the property in 1905, the building became the Blue Ridge Hotel. Finally, in 1910, it was sold to Mayberry I. Patterson, who gave the hotel his surname. The building, still standing, has been redesigned to accommodate students from the nearby university center. (Courtesy of David Wiles.)

In the post–Civil War era, Hagerstown entered a period of strong economic growth. As a transportation hub, the city was in need of additional hostelries to accommodate the increasing number of travelers. The Hotel Hamilton was constructed by former governor, US senator, and congressman William T. Hamilton in the mid-1880s during a hotel-building boom. The building has changed hands and usage several times, and its vocation is now in a state of transition. (Courtesy of Western Maryland Historical Library.)

The Gateway Inn, located along the pike between Hagerstown and Clear Spring, was a stop for weary travelers on the old National Pike. It was built in the early to mid-1800s, probably as a stone structure, and was expanded a number of times. It remained a restaurant until recently and still stands as an example of an old pike hostelry. (Courtesy of Clear Spring Historical Association.)

All too often, automobiles traveling the National Road in the first half of the 1900s took unwanted rest stops. Drivers facing flat tires, overheated engines, or mechanical breakdowns could attempt a do-it-yourself fix or assistance from the nearest service station. In the early days of automobile touring along the pike, it was wise practice to carry tools and extra gasoline, since places to find help were often few and far between. In this photograph, taken west of Hagerstown, the woman appears to be the car's driver, and her perplexed stance indicates that the car may have failed her. (Courtesy of University of Milwaukee Library.)

Travelers along the Washington County portion of the National Pike in April 1905 were witnesses to a revolutionary development. A wagon with cabinet-type doors, drawn by two horses, made its way along the pike. Behind those cabinet doors was a miniature library with a variety of books to be offered for loan to residents throughout the county. This curiosity was the first bookmobile in the United States. It was inaugurated by Mary Titcomb, Washington County Free Library's first librarian, and utilized the National Pike and other county roads to promote book reading. The concept soon spread to other parts of the United States. (Courtesy of Western Maryland Historical Library.)

The National Pike is dotted with historical roadside markers highlighting significant sites and events. The statewide program began in 1933 under the auspices of the Maryland State Roads Commission. This marker is located on the National Road between Hagerstown and Clear Spring. The photograph was taken in 1937 and summarizes the history of the Bank Road, financed by Maryland banks to fill the gap in roadways between the west end of the Wilson Bridge and Cumberland. The 40-mile stretch was constructed between 1816 and 1821. (Courtesy of Maryland Historical Trust.)

While there was some improvement of roads in the waning years of the 1800s, many remained in poor condition as the 20th century arrived. Loose dirt turned to mud after rainstorms, and potholes rutted many roads after winter passed. As increasing numbers of Americans were able to afford automobiles, the demand for good roads turned into a widespread call to action. The Good Roads Movement began with the bicyclists of the late 1880s and gained enough influence by 1912 to spur Congressional passage of a bill to improve postal roads and, in 1916, the Good Roads Act. The latter broadened federal financing and was followed in 1921 by a further expansion of funding and national highway development. The National Road was a major beneficiary of these advancements. The photographs above and below show the results of these developments. Each was taken in the same stretch of road leading to the National Road's bridge across the Conococheague Creek, about seven miles west of Hagerstown. The vast improvement of the road between 1898 and 1930 is evident. (Both, courtesy of Maryland State Roads Commission.)

The bridge over the Conococheague Creek, about seven miles from Hagerstown, was another example of the classic stone arch bridges built along the National Pike in Maryland. The five-arch Wilson Bridge (background), so-called because of its proximity to the little village of the same name, was built in 1819. It was replaced in the 1930s with a modern structure (foreground) and continued in use until 1972. The old bridge remains and serves as a living reminder of the majestic stone architecture of the crossings on the original National Road. (Courtesy of Clear Spring Historical Association.)

The area adjacent to the old Wilson Bridge started out as a mill, built around the time the bridge was constructed. George W. Row purchased the property in 1923 and removed the mill and other old buildings to make room for a large amusement park and summer cottages. The park operated into the 1960s and is now an automobile racetrack. As can be seen in the photograph, summer visitors sometimes used the bridge as a lounging area overlooking the bathing beach below. (Courtesy of Albert and Angela Feldstein.)

The tiny former village of Wilson stands on the west side of the Conococheague bridge. The country store, built in the 1850s by Rufus H. Wilson, sits along the original National Pike alignment and has been restored. The post office that was located inside the store also has been restored, along with a one-room schoolhouse. Rufus Wilson lost his wife and two of his children in the early 1850s. He constructed the schoolhouse in 1855 for his remaining son and local children. (Courtesy of David Wiles.)

The National Road in Maryland was noted for its dangerous curves in both its horse-drawn and automobile years. This accident, however, seems to have occurred on a straight portion of the road between Hagerstown and Clear Spring, underscoring that, as on any thoroughfare, other factors often contribute to mishaps. (Courtesy of Farm Security Administration.)

The diminutive hamlet of Shady Bower was both a popular and unpopular stopping point along the pike. Weary travelers could find refreshment and respite at Conrad Wolsey's convivial tavern. But first they were required to stop at the tollhouse and pay a tariff to continue their journey. In the c. 1891 photograph above, the people flanking the Shady Bower toll keeper are probably family members. If they are all sharing space in the tollhouse, one hopes that they are close-knit and easygoing. Down the road, Wolsey's Tavern is no doubt burnishing its fine reputation. In his 1894 recollections, Thomas Searight reported that Conrad's enterprise "was well favored by wagoners, who sought his generous board in goodly numbers, and . . . was well liked by his customers." Conveniently, a large distillery operated near the tavern. Notwithstanding the popularity of his establishment, Wolsey bore the nickname "Dirty Spigot" after the tap on a whiskey barrel was found to be "besmeared with filth." The building remains standing and is now a private residence (below). (Above, courtesy of Western Maryland Room, Washington County Free Library; below, courtesy of Babs Savitt.)

Travel on the National Road by coaches and other multi-passenger vehicles declined drastically after the railroad reached Cumberland in 1852. It was partially revived near the turn of the 20th century when intercity buses began plying the road. In 1893, Lewis H. Blair inaugurated bus transportation between Clear Spring and Hagerstown. A 1901 newspaper article under the headline "Business Booms" reported that Blair had purchased "a very pretty wagon of the latest design, and of up-to-date construction, with glass front, this affording a much-needed protection against the weather." He also increased the pulling power by adding a second horse. Motorized vehicles soon replaced the horses. In addition to intercity transportation, Blair offered sightseeing excursions. In 1923, he purchased a new limousine bus manufactured by premier vehicle maker Fageol Motors. In the undated photograph above, one of Lewis Blair's motorbuses is proudly displayed. Below, a group of excursionists is about to depart Clear Spring in one of the company's open-air buses. (Both, courtesy of Clear Spring Historical Association.)

POTOMAC HOUSE, CLEARSPRING, WASHINGTON CO. MD
F. FELLINGER & SON, PROPRIETORS.

In 1776, Jacob Myers, a resident of Lancaster, Pennsylvania, was given a sizable plot of land in settlement of a debt. The land was not developed until 1790, when it was subdivided among a son and two daughters. They each built homes and farmed the land. In 1821, with the new National Road running through the settlement, Jacob's son Martin mapped out lots along the road and applied for recognition of his new town, Myersville. Martin built a stone and log store in what was to become the center of town. Local lore professes that a flowing, clear spring in front of the house was the inspiration for the renaming of the town. Soon after Clear Spring's establishment, the American Hotel was constructed on Cumberland Street—the main street and the path of the National Road. Henry Clay was a frequent guest of the hotel on his many trips between his home in Lexington, Kentucky, and the nation's capital. The establishment's name was changed in the 1870s to the Potomac House. The building was eventually converted into a private dwelling and still stands. (Courtesy of Clear Spring Historical Association.)

In 1884, two brothers from Ohio traveled east to tour the Civil War sites in Virginia, West Virginia, and Maryland. One of the brothers was an amateur photographer and brought his equipment along on the journey. The photograph above was taken as the brothers approached Clear Spring from the east. (Courtesy of Western Maryland Historical Library.)

Almost all the buildings on the pike (Cumberland Street) in Clear Spring housed businesses at one point. Many of the structures remain today, but most have been converted into private dwellings. Identifiable enterprises in this early-1900s photograph include S.N. Hull's barbershop (see the sign on the first building at left), a gas station (note the gas pump in the middle of the photograph), and a confectionery (behind and to the left of the gas pump). Judging by the picture, bike riding was a popular pastime in town. (Courtesy of Clear Spring Historical Association.)

Spickler's gas station began its life in the 1800s as a blacksmith and carriage-making shop along the National Pike. John Carbaugh Sr., a lifelong Clear Spring resident, farmer, teacher, and shop owner, recalled in his memoir that a promotional pocket mirror was given out by Spickler's. On the back was a ditty whose first verse said: "If you've got a Spickler buggy / And your best girl's with you then, / You've got a right to feel contented / And the proudest of all men." With the advent of the automobile age, Spickler's became a service station and Ford dealership. (Courtesy of Julie and Ken Carbaugh and the Clear Spring Historical Association.)

The village of Indian Springs sits four miles west of Clear Spring along the pike. While the who and when of the community's naming appears to remain a mystery, it is clear that the growth of the area coincided with the early success of the National Road. The Indian Springs Store (above, on the left) sold a bit of everything and housed a tailor shop in the back and, probably, the village post office. During the Depression of the 1930s, the owner organized square dances and hosted boxing matches to make ends meet. Throughout its history, the Indian Springs Store served as a gathering place for local citizens to exchange news and gossip and solve the problems of the world. (Courtesy of Clear Spring Historical Association.)

There are indications that the Indian Springs Hotel existed prior to the construction of the National Road. The hostelry changed ownership a number of times during the 19th century but never stopped offering travelers lodging, a meal, and a drink or two of locally produced whiskey. As with other enterprises along the road, business declined significantly during the second half of the 1800s and rebounded with the coming of the automobile age. A newspaper review in 1925 reported that "it is one place where the desire for real American food can be thoroughly satisfied." Despite Prohibition, it appears that patrons also were able to procure an outlawed glass of whiskey. On at least three occasions, the proprietors were arrested and indicted for serving alcohol. (Courtesy of Clear Spring Historical Association.)

In this 1884 photograph, a tollhouse stands a small distance west of the Indian Springs Hotel. The tollgate is raised, and farther down the road, a covered bridge is visible. During the final quarter of the 19th century, the National Road was in serious decline, and the roadbed, as evidenced in this photograph, was a virtual dirt track in many places. (Courtesy of Western Maryland Historical Library.)

The hamlet of Millstone cannot even be called a ghost town. There is virtually nothing left of this tiny but once busy "pike town." The National Road, which used to run through the main street, has been realigned and completely bypasses the site of the town. A flood in 1924 caused the closure of the canal. The construction of Interstate 70 in the early 1960s put the finishing touches on the demise of the town. The Chesapeake & Ohio Canal, of course, remains nearby, but there are no residents to walk along its towpath. The railroad tracks are the only "living" transportation path through what was once Millstone. In the early 1900s, the town had a population of approximately 100 people and was served by two general stores, a hotel, church, school, post office, shoe shop, and railroad stop. The undated photograph above shows the heart of "downtown" Millstone. The Millstone Hotel, seen in the photograph below, often housed railroad employees and later became a residence before its demise. (Above, courtesy of *Cracker Barrel* magazine; below, courtesy of Hancock Historical Society.)

The National Road's sovereignty lasted until the mid-19th century. On July 4, 1828, construction of the Chesapeake & Ohio Canal began in Washington, DC, with a grand ceremony featuring Pres. John Quincy Adams shoveling the first spadeful of dirt. On that same day, 40 miles north, Charles Carroll—one of the last living signers of the Declaration of Independence—helped lay the cornerstone that marked the beginning of construction of the Baltimore & Ohio Railroad. The canal was completed to Cumberland in 1850. It was intended to continue to the Ohio River, but the difficulty and expense of construction led to the abandonment of these plans. Meanwhile, the B&O Railroad was making steady progress. It reached Cumberland in 1842 and Wheeling in 1853. The railroad's speed and carrying capacity made it the preferred means of travel for people and most goods. The Chesapeake & Ohio Canal remained in operation until 1924, primarily carrying coal. The National Road, too, quickly lost favor in wake of the railroad's advantages. The three means of transportation can be seen in each of these photographs, taken between Hagerstown and Hancock. (Above, courtesy of Library of Congress; below, author's collection.)

Hancock became a town when Edward Joseph Hancock laid out lots in 1749. The area had been called Great North Bend by local Native Americans and Tonoloway Settlement by early settlers before taking the name of the town's founder. The construction of the Bank Road and its coupling with the Cumberland Road in 1818 brought an influx of traffic, businesses, and new settlers to Hancock as it became a "pike town." It became a "canal town" as well when the Chesapeake & Ohio Canal reached Hancock in 1839. Both the National Road (center) and the Chesapeake & Ohio Canal are visible in this bird's-eye view of the town. (Courtesy of Albert and Angela Feldstein.)

In 1879, during the National Road's years of obsolescence, William H. Rideing described Hancock as "lugubriously apathetic." In the late 1800s, Edmund Pendleton Cohill established a commercial apple orchard near town, and Hancock soon developed into a major fruit producer. With the revival of the National Road and the continued importance of cement production, the municipality became what was described in the *Maryland Cracker Barrel* magazine as "the busiest little town in Maryland." The image above shows a portion of Baltimore Street (the National Road) around 1906. (Courtesy of Albert and Angela Feldstein.)

In 1902, and on many occasions before and after, heavy rain caused the Potomac River to overflow its banks around Hancock. The National Road became a mud bog in many places. Baltimore Street (the National Road) was hard hit, as is evident in this photograph. (Courtesy of Washington County Historical Society.)

Travelers on the National Pike in April 1937 were probably startled to see a dogsled team barreling down the road. A year earlier, Patrick J. Carroll—a 45-year-old author, gold prospector, and hunting guide—set out with his wife and a team of six dogs on a 6,000-mile trek from Ootsa Lake, British Columbia, to Halifax, Nova Scotia. A seventh dog, Spareribs, served as backup. The team, led by a veteran canine named Wolf, pulled a sled outfitted with rubber-tired wheels. Each of the dogs was part wolf and part St. Bernard and wore protective moccasins. The arctic squad averaged 12 to 20 miles a day. By the time they reached Maryland, they had worn out 3,000 pairs of shoes. In the above photograph, the team is seen congregating with local citizens in Hancock. (Courtesy of Hancock Historical Society.)

One of the favored stops along the pike during its heyday was Benjamin Bean's inn and tavern in Hancock. A traveler writing in an 1879 issue of *Harper's Monthly* lamented the saloon's transformation into a boardinghouse run by "two precise and elderly nieces" of Bean. The fondly remembered establishment welcomed a wide variety of "thirsty and exhausted traveler[s]," who enjoyed "the tinkling of glasses and the hearty interchange of greetings and compliments that enlivened the room." Among the clients were a number of contemporary celebrities, including Andrew Jackson, Henry Clay, Davy Crockett, William Henry Harrison, Zachary Taylor, and James K. Polk. In the scene above, Andrew Jackson is receiving a welcoming speech from a local dignitary in the Barton House during the presidential campaign of 1832. The hostelry (below) continued to serve travelers until 1905, when it became a store. Today, the building houses the Hancock Visitor's Center. (Above, courtesy of *Harper's Monthly*, author's collection; below, courtesy of Hancock Historical Society.)

One of the few original tollhouses remaining on the pike stands on the western outskirts of Hancock. The structure was built around 1820. It has survived for another century and serves as a nostalgic artifact of the old National Road. (Courtesy of Hancock Historical Society.)

"Old Mr. Flint's Home," located a short distance from the old tollhouse, dates from the mid- to late 1700s. The original log house has been significantly enlarged over the years and covered with stucco. It was built by a Native American named Joseph Flint, who was a friend or acquaintance of George Washington. The nation's first president visited the area in 1769 and recorded in his diary that "Old Mr. Flint dined with us." Five days later, he wrote of a visit to Flint's home. The Cohill family later acquired the home, and in 1886, E.P. Cohill, the "Father of Maryland's Apple Industry," planted his first 40 acres of apples in the area. The home remains a private residence. (Courtesy of Western Maryland Room, Washington County Free Library.)

Sideling Hill was one of the most feared sections of the National Road in Maryland because of its rapid rise and descent, combined with horseshoe and S curves. On the eastern side of the hill, about seven miles west of Hancock, the road climbed 760 feet in 1.5 miles. On the western slope, travelers descended 495 feet during a one-mile stretch. Robert Bruce describing an excursion along the pike in 1915 warned motorists descending the western slope to coast "with the brake on lightly, not only on account of the grade, but especially to prepare for the very sharp curve—almost a 'horseshoe'—at the foot." The image above was taken at the edge of one of Sideling's many curves. In the 1960s, the perils of crossing Sideling Hill were virtually eliminated by the construction of Interstate 68. The cut made through Sideling revealed a fascinating rainbow of strata and a story of thousands of years of geological development (below). (Both, courtesy of Albert and Angela Feldstein.)

The rising popularity of bicycles fostered a national movement to improve roads in the 1880s. The advent of the automobile age around the turn of the 20th century led to an increased awareness of the need for smooth, durable roads. Within a decade, this had blossomed into the nationwide Good Roads Movement. Groups sprang up across the country to lobby federal and state governments to fund road improvements. A 1914 publication used the above photograph—taken on a stretch of road between Hancock and Cumberland—to underscore the problem. (Courtesy of Frostburg University Library.)

Although far from being the highest mountain on Maryland's National Pike, Polish Mountain provided travelers with majestic views of the mountains of western Maryland, Pennsylvania, and West Virginia. To get an even better view, travelers could climb the steps to the observation tower at the crest of Polish Mountain. The tower stood at the back of Yonker's, a popular rest stop on the way to or from Cumberland. From the 1920s to the 1950s, Yonker's offered meals, souvenirs, pottery, baths, and gasoline. (Courtesy of Albert and Angela Feldstein.)

The Flintstone Hotel in the little village of the same name was built in 1807 and served travelers on what was to become the National Road. John Piper, head clerk at the nearby John Davis store, ultimately acquired the store, the surrounding farm, and the tavern, which became the Piper House hostelry. In addition to journeyers on the pike, the Piper House's guests included patrons of Flintstone's warm springs. The establishment became the Flintstone Hotel under the proprietorship of the town's physician, A.T. Twigg. During its more than 100 years of operation, the inn was visited by luminaries such as General Lafayette, Grover Cleveland, and Henry Clay. (Courtesy of Albert and Angela Feldstein.)

"City Digs Self Out of Worst Flood in History." Travelers heading from Flintstone to Cumberland on March 30, 1924, did not need to read the headline on page one of the *Cumberland Evening Times* to know what was before them. The *Times* reported that the devastating flood was caused by the rapid melting of the heavy accumulations of snow in the surrounding mountains, unleashed by two days of warm rains. The National Road through the city was not spared, as can be seen in this photograph of Baltimore Street. (Courtesy of Maryland State Archives.)

Five

You Must Go Over, You Cannot Go Around

Cumberland to the Mason-Dixon Line

Travel on the western Maryland portion of the old National Road was not for the faint of heart or for those with a fear of heights. Even in the era of the Good Roads Movement, more than 100 years after the Cumberland Road was laid out, an undulating trip over the Maryland mountains could seem both daunting and exhilarating. The adventure was compounded by a profusion of twists, turns, and horseshoe curves. And, as the popular *Mohawk-Hobbs Guide* reminded travelers in the 1920s, "You must go over—You cannot go around."

There was one exception to the guide's admonishment. In its first 15 years, heading west from Cumberland, the old road immediately climbed and descended Wills Mountain. In 1833, authorization was granted to utilize a route discovered 78 years earlier by one of General Braddock's officers. While less formidable than the original route, this more circular artery led through some intimidating territory. A stagecoach passenger in 1840, William H. Wills, reported that the road through the fabled Narrows "presents a solemn and stupendous spectacle" of rocks resting on rocks that seem "almost ready to tumble down upon and crush [the traveler] to atoms."

After passing through the Narrows, journeyers faced a ceaseless series of steep ascents and intimidating descents. Englishman William Faux, traveling by mail coach in 1819, complained that "All here is wild, awfully precipitous, and darkly umbrageous, high as the heavens, or low as perdition." The climbs were laborious but not nearly as dicey as the downgrades, where the combination of speed (sometimes uncontrolled) and braking power could lead to lamentable outcomes.

The reward for accepting these discomforts and dangers was experiencing the incredible scenery and mountaintop vistas. Ohio congressman Albert Douglas, traveling home with his wife along the pike in 1909, complained bitterly about the condition of the road but tempered his anger as he observed the terrain: "When we came to the summit [of Big Savage Mountain], and caught the glorious view to the West and Southwest, of meadows, fields, woods, and piled up mountains our discomfort vanished."

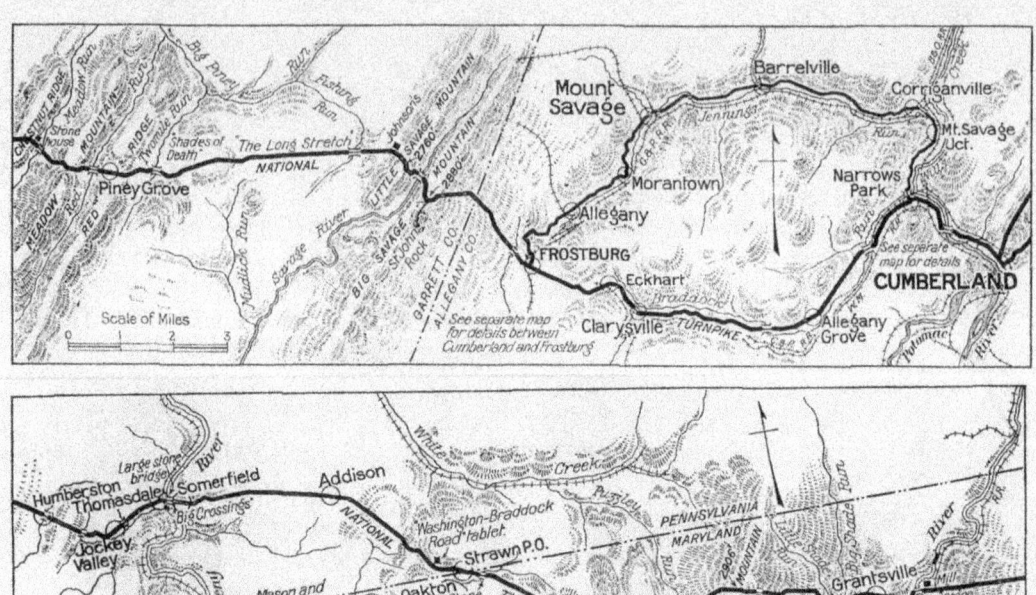

The "new" route west from Cumberland, laid out in 1833, avoided a direct crossing of Wills Mountain, but the highest mountains along the pike were still ahead. Though often unnerved by the many dangers, journeyers were awed by the spectacular scenery and often recorded their reactions in journals, articles, and books. After conquering the highest peak, Negro Mountain, the National Road made its way out of Maryland and into Pennsylvania. (Courtesy of Robert Bruce, *The National Road*, author's collection.)

FORT CUMBERLAND 1755.
From foot of Nobley.

In 1753, Virginia lieutenant governor Robert Dinwiddie sent a small force headed by George Washington to demand that French forces withdraw from territory in the Ohio Valley. The mission failed, and in early 1754, Washington was ordered to return and remove the French by force. This too failed, and Washington suffered defeat at the hastily built Fort Necessity in Pennsylvania. The British forces retreated to the area that is now Cumberland and constructed Fort Mount Pleasant. It was soon renamed Fort Cumberland in honor of King George II's third son. In 1755, Fort Cumberland served as the jumping off point for Gen. Edward Braddock's army in its unsuccessful expedition against the French at Fort Duquesne (now Pittsburgh). Little more than a thin path existed between Forts Cumberland and Duquesne. In order to move his army and all its equipment, Braddock had to widen the narrow trail to create a road. Fifty years later, the new National Pike generally paralleled this byway. The painting above depicts the fort in 1755. The sketch below was drawn by George Washington. Note the dotted lines of the trail to Fort Duquesne. (Above, courtesy of Albert and Angela Feldstein; below, courtesy of Library of Congress.)

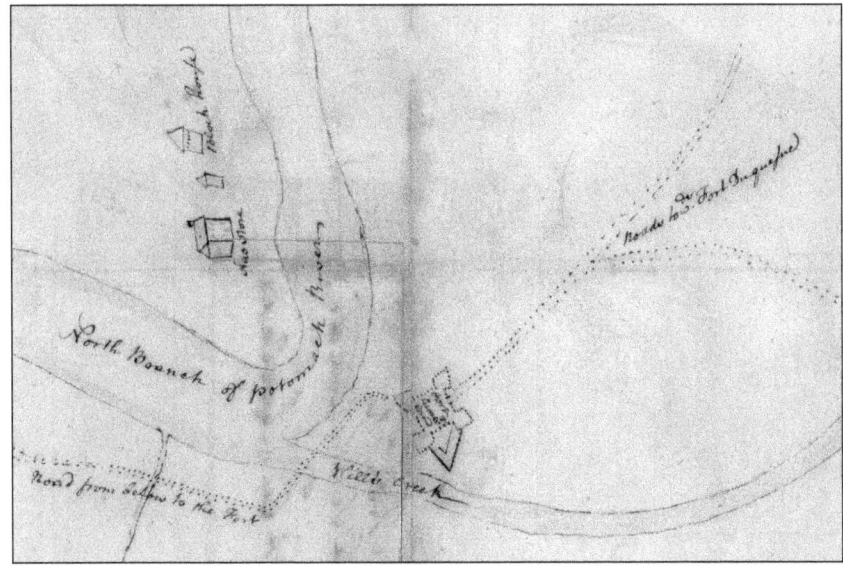

The privately owned portion of the National Road connected in Cumberland with the beginning of the section financed by the federal government. Thirty years after the establishment of Fort Cumberland, Thomas Beall, a Revolutionary War veteran, laid out plots to create a village. In 1787, the Maryland Legislature passed an act of incorporation creating the town of Cumberland. The fledgling municipality benefitted from the development of immense coal deposits in the surrounding area. The construction of the National Pike and the subsequent creation of the Chesapeake & Ohio Canal and a railroad line from the east spurred rapid growth. Cumberland became the second-largest manufacturing center in Maryland, topped only by Baltimore. In the photograph above, the National Road wends its way through the eastern outskirts of Cumberland in the late 1940s. In the image of Baltimore Street below, the Emmanuel Protestant Episcopal Church on the site of Fort Cumberland is visible in the distance. (Above, courtesy of Albert and Angela Feldstein; below, courtesy of the Maryland Department, Enoch Pratt Free Library/Maryland's State Library Resource Center.)

In its report to Pres. Thomas Jefferson, the commission assigned to lay out the Cumberland Pike designated a spot near the confluence of the Potomac River and Wills Creek as the road's starting point. Writing in 1916, Robert Bruce identified an area along present-day Green Street as Mile 0 of the pike. Referencing the 1909 photograph above, Bruce reported that the actual site of the ground-breaking probably was in the area opposite the curve in the trolley tracks. To reach this point coming from the east, travelers had to ford Wills Creek until a bridge was constructed. The original ford was filled in to create Riverside Park. In 2012, a monument was erected to mark the starting point of the pike. The route west from Cumberland took travelers over rough, mountainous terrain, greatly slowing down travel and posing a danger to travelers. Consequently, in 1833, a new route was laid out that, without markedly adding time, took travelers on a circuitous but much easier course to a point six miles west of Cumberland, where it rejoined the pike (see map). (Both, courtesy of Robert Bruce, *The National Road*, author's collection.)

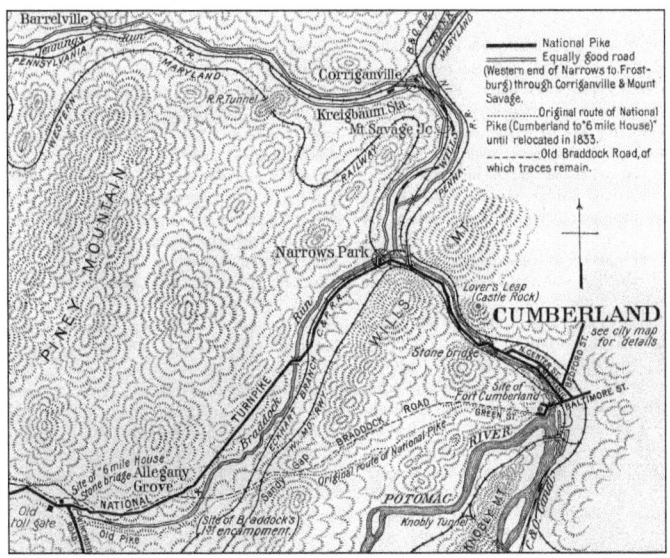

The commissioners charged with planning the Cumberland Road were required to find the straightest route possible. The first hurdle they encountered was Wills Mountain. Located less than a mile west of Cumberland, the mountain stood 1,877 feet high. Its rugged, tree-lined terrain posed a significant challenge to road builders. The image above gives an idea of the difficulties facing planners and laborers as they began construction of the new road. The trail paralleled the route of the Braddock expedition's attempt to cross over Wills Mountain through Sandy Gap in 1755. (Courtesy of Frostburg State University Library.)

The route leading to Wills Mountain along the National Road (Baltimore Street) crossed Washington Street and Wills Creek before beginning the ascent to Sandy Gap. In the above photograph, taken in the late 1800s, the bridge in the center had long supplanted the ford over the creek. The bridge leads to the nearby starting point of the original Cumberland Road. (Courtesy of Albert and Angela Feldstein.)

Cumberland's Baltimore Street was a bustling sea of people and vehicles during the National Road's primacy. Despite the opening of the rail line to Baltimore in 1842 and, to a much lesser extent, the completion of the Chesapeake & Ohio Canal in 1850, the National Road remained a viable thoroughfare for a number of years. In 1848, stagecoaches transported 2,586 passengers along the pike through the city. But the road ceased being the dominant means of transportation eastward and westward. The city remained a transportation center by dint of its location. With the success of the coal industry and the establishment of manufacturing enterprises, Cumberland continued to grow. One of the oldest photographs of the city, taken in 1858, shows a busy Baltimore Street lined with shops (above), as does a later photograph from around the turn of the 20th century (below). (Both, courtesy of Albert and Angela Feldstein.)

An area called the Narrows sits along the 1833 route of the National Pike, beginning one mile northwest of Cumberland. This nine-mile-long gorge, wedged between high cliffs, divides Wills Mountain in two. In an 1857 article in *Harper's Monthly*, Brantz Mayer, a well-known writer at the time, described the Narrows as "this wilderness of romantic disorder." Gen. Zachary Taylor was spellbound as he passed through the area on the way to his presidential inauguration. Thomas Searight recorded that Taylor passed through the Narrows at twilight and ordered his party to stop. "Out he got in the storm and snow and looked at the giddy heights on either side of Wills Creek until he had taken in the grandeur of the scenery." Photographers have long labored to capture the beauty of the area and transfer it to postcards and photograph prints. The image above represents one of those attempts. As evident in the photograph at left, taken in 1906, the natural beauty was challenged by the introduction of the National Road and later by railroad and trolley lines. (Above, courtesy of Western Maryland Historical Library; left, courtesy of Angela and Albert Feldstein.)

The Narrows, like many other mountainous areas, has long had a "Lover's Leap," named for a heartbroken person's 1,000-foot leap to the bottom of the gorge. And like other Lover's Leaps, commercial enterprises sprang up to offer tourists and other passersby a bit of sustenance, gasoline, and the opportunity to purchase must-have souvenirs. At one time a hostelry, the Wills Mountain Inn, stood at the top of the mountain near Lover's Leap. Travelers could reach the inn by way of a winding road from the Narrows to the summit. (Courtesy of Albert and Angela Feldstein.)

A person need not be a heartbroken suitor to climb to the top of Lover's Leap. Most adventurers who have labored to reach the peak were seeking a beautiful view of the spectacular scenery in and around the deep gorge. And, of course, there were some (left) who could not resist the challenge of reaching an outcropping and dangling a leg or two over the sheer edge. (Courtesy of Albert and Angela Feldstein.)

The original Cumberland Road and the longer-but-easier 1833 artery were rejoined approximately six miles west of Cumberland. In this photograph, taken in 1884, the photographer was standing on the old road. The edge of that road is visible, as is the new road in the center and to the left side of the image. (Courtesy of Western Maryland Historical Library.)

When the State of Maryland agreed to the change of route west from Cumberland in 1833, it insisted that the federal government macadamize the new roadway, construct a strong stone bridge over Wills Creek in the Narrows, and build equally sturdy and durable bridges where necessary along the pike. The attractive stone bridge pictured above was one of the results of the agreement. It has carried traffic for over 185 years. (Courtesy of Virginia Williams Kelly.)

Few tollhouses remain from the halcyon years of the old National Pike. The first tollhouse on Maryland's section of the road was constructed six miles west of Cumberland in what is now the town of LaVale. It began operating soon after Maryland took ownership of the road from the federal government and remained active until the early 20th century. Its seven-sided design was repeated in many of the other tollhouses along the pike. In 1913, the LaVale tollhouse was sold by the State of Maryland to a private individual. After passing through several owners, including, again, the State of Maryland, it fell into disrepair. The tollhouse was restored in the 1960s and remains open for tours. In the photograph above, taken between 1891 and 1901, writer Robert Bruce identifies the man sitting under the overhang as "Mr. Cady . . . the last keeper to collect tolls." In the etching at right, published in 1879, the driver of the "express" Conestoga wagon appears to have paid the toll and is ready to proceed on his westward journey. (Above, courtesy of Robert Bruce, *The National Road*, author's collection; right, courtesy of *Harper's Monthly*, author's collection.)

TOLL RATES

Forevery score of Sheep or Hogs.	6 cents
Forevery score of Cattle.	12 cents
Forevery Horse and Rider.	4 cents
Forevery led or driven Horse, Mule or Ass.	3 cents
Forevery Sleigh or Sled drawn by one horse or pair of Oxen.	3 cents
Forevery Horse or pair of Oxen in Addition.	3 cents
Forevery Dearborn, Sulky, Chair or Chaise with one horse.	6 cents
Forevery Horse in Addition.	3 cents
Forevery Chariot, Coach, Cochee, Stage, Phaeton or Chaise with two Horses and four wheels.	12 cents
Forevery Carriage of pleasure by whatever be it called the same according to the number of wheels and horses drawing the same.	
Forevery Cart or Wagon whose wheels do not exceed three inches in breadth, drawn by horse or pair of Oxen.	4 cents
Forevery Cart or wagon whose wheels exceed three inches and does not exceed four inches in breadth for every horse or pair of oxen drawing the same.	4 cents
Wheels exceeding four and not exceeding six inches.	3 cents
Wheels exceeding six and not exceeding eight inches.	2 cents
All Carts or Wagons whose wheels exceed eight inches in breadth. Free.	

DAVID T. SHRIVER, Supt.

Toll rates were based on the type and quantity of animals being herded and/or the type of vehicle. The image at left is a facsimile of the sign that was displayed at the LaVale tollhouse. In the case of carts or wagons, the distance separating the wheels determined the amount of the toll. The wider the separation, the lower the tariff. While this may seem counterintuitive, the reasoning was that a narrow breadth of wheels did more damage to the road than a wider breadth. The person whose name appears at the bottom of the sign, David T. Shriver, was the first superintendent of the Cumberland Road. He served from 1811 to 1820. The superintendent's responsibilities included finding, hiring, and supervising contractors; ensuring that building supplies were onsite; and ensuring that the contractors and laborers were keeping to schedule. (Courtesy of Jordan Savitt.)

Journeyers attempting to evade the toll stations would exit the road a hidden distance away and follow a circuitous route before rejoining the road beyond the tollgate. In Benevola, near Hagerstown, the diversionary road has endured to this day and is named Tollpass Lane. (Courtesy of Babs Savitt.)

Clarysville (above) arose because of its location on the Cumberland Road and the area's mining heritage. The village has never had a large population, but through the years, it was a consistently popular stopping point for travelers and in the late 1800s a small bedroom community for mine employees. The star attraction for pike journeyers was the Clarysville Inn. Built in 1807, it was located eight miles west of Cumberland. The inn was built by Gerard Clary, a Baltimore County native who married the daughter of the property's owner. His nephew Aden took over the inn when Gerard died in 1851. Thomas Searight recalled that "there was not a more popular house on the road than Adam [sic] Cleary's." In the 1884 photograph below, the pike is in the foreground, and the inn is at the far end of the road. While there were several relatively minor changes to the outer structure, the hostelry retained its overall appearance throughout its 142-year life. It was destroyed by fire in 1999. (Above, courtesy of Virginia Williams Kelly; below, courtesy of Western Maryland Historical Library.)

CLARYSVILLE GENERAL HOSPITAL, U.S.A., 1864, BETWEEN FROSTBURG AND CUMBERLAND, MD.

Clarysville is best known as the site of a large hospital complex during the Civil War. In the war's early months, wounded soldiers, mostly Union but some Confederates, were housed in makeshift quarters in Cumberland. The city's accessibility by road, railroad, and canal made it seem a convenient location for ministering to casualties of battle. Cumberland, however, was ill-suited to this role. Its hot summers and insufficient facilities led to a search for a more favorable location. Mary Townsend, the wife of Dr. Morris Miller Townsend, a civilian doctor working for the Union army, came up with a solution. "I knew of the very place, eight and one-half miles from Cumberland, in a delightful valley . . . [with] the finest spring water, a large wagon tavern [the Clarysville Inn], several houses and three barns not used for years." After a careful inspection, Clarysville was deemed a suitable site, and construction began immediately. The medical center ministered to an average of 1,000–1,500 patients and, at times, as many as 2,000. The Clarysville Inn stood within the compound and served as officer's quarters as well as a hospital. The complex operated from 1862 to 1864 and, aside from the inn, was dismantled after the war. (Author's collection.)

The town of Eckhart Mines was laid out in 1789 by George Eckhart, a German immigrant. Coal mining began in the early 1800s, and when large-scale operations were launched in the 1830s, Eckhart Mines became the first coal company town in Maryland. The location on the National Road contributed to the early success of the mining operations. The photograph above shows the National Road as it traversed Eckhart Mines in the early 1900s. (Courtesy of Virginia Williams Kelly.)

Although railway lines had served Eckhart Mines since the 1840s, it was not until 1902 that passenger trolley service was inaugurated. The *Cumberland Times* reported that the Frostburg-Eckhart-Cumberland Electric Railway "should provide low cost transportation for citizens and increase trade and business." The trolley ran along the edge of the National Road between the three towns. It left every hour on the hour until 10:00 p.m. and took 40 minutes to travel between Cumberland and Frostburg. The photograph above was taken in the 1920s. (Courtesy of Albert and Angela Feldstein.)

Frostburg was the first stop for stagecoaches heading west on the National Road from Cumberland. The 10-mile stretch of road rises from 627 feet above sea level to 2,070 feet as it reaches Frostburg on its ascent of Big Savage Mountain. In this 1884 photograph, the city can be seen in the distance as the road levels out and passes through it heading west before making the final climb to the peak of the mountain. (Courtesy of Western Maryland Historical Library.)

Frostburg's first high school was built on this site overlooking the city. The original Beall High School was established in the mid-1890s and stood southwest of downtown Frostburg as the city grew around it. This photograph was taken around the 1880s or early 1890s. (Courtesy of Frostburg State University Library.)

The area that would become the city of Frostburg was a tiny settlement until plans for the Cumberland Road made clear that the road would pass directly through it. Josiah Frost had settled in the area at the end of the 18th century and acquired a large tract of land. His son Meshach inherited a portion of this land and in 1812 built a home in what is now downtown Frostburg. Construction of the new road from Cumberland to Frostburg was completed in 1812. As expected, it became a major thoroughfare and brought many travelers through the area. Meshach opened a tavern, Highland Hall, and set up a community named Mount Pleasant. Locals called the burgeoning town "Frost's Town," and in 1820, when a post office was established, the new name was adopted. It became Frostburg when the town was incorporated in 1878. When coal mining became a major industry in the 1830s, Frostburg experienced another growth spurt. The photographs of Main Street (National Road) date from the early 1900s. (Above, courtesy of Albert and Angela Feldstein; below, courtesy of Virginia Williams Kelly.)

Road conditions along the National Road in the early 1900s, already problematic in many places, were greatly affected by the weather. In this photograph, heavy snowfall in February 1910 clogged Frostburg's Main Street and severely hindered travel on the pike. (Courtesy of Frostburg State University Library.)

The Hotel Gladstone opened on January 1, 1897 (see architect's drawing above). It was located on Main Street in Frostburg and, according to the Maryland Inventory of Historic Properties, "was constructed . . . to provide both entertainment and lodging to persons traveling the National Road." The Gladstone had 100 rooms, a barbershop, a café, tennis courts, a petting zoo, and an observatory. Unfortunately, the hotel was unsuccessful, and in 1903, it was sold to William Gunter, who installed electric lighting and a 175-seat dining room and renamed it the Hotel Gunter. In subsequent years, it was home to a speakeasy, a cockfighting arena, and a jail. The latter was housed in the basement to quarter convicts being transported to prison. In 2018, the hotel was purchased by a Frostburg city councilman and his wife, who intend to use it as a restaurant, distillery, and tasting room, while offering several guest rooms to rent. (Courtesy of Frostburg State University Library.)

This was the second toll station traveling west from Cumberland. It was located seven miles from the LaVale tollhouse, near the border between Allegany and Garrett Counties. When this photograph was taken in 1907, automobile travel had not yet eclipsed horse-drawn vehicles, although the electric railway between Cumberland, Eckhart, and Frostburg provided an alternative for local travelers. (Courtesy of Albert and Angela Feldstein.)

Travelers leaving Frostburg in the first decade of the 20th century faced many stretches where poor surfacing made for a bumpy ride. This photograph of the National Road on the outskirts of Frostburg provides an idea of the type of roadway that fostered breakdowns and subjected journeyers to an uncomfortable trip. (Courtesy of Virginia Williams Kelly.)

An ascent of St. John's Rock, near the peak of Big Savage Mountain, took adventurers to an altitude of 2,930 feet. Following his 1915 tour of the National Road from Baltimore to Wheeling, West Virginia, Robert Bruce opined that "the view from St. John's Rock is probably the finest on this trip." As seen in this image, excursioners could climb the rocks to experience this view. (Courtesy of Frostburg State University Library.)

Less adventurous tourists could still enjoy a stunning view if they followed the pike to the top of Big Savage Mountain. At 2,850 feet, visitors could see for many miles in all directions. Big Savage Mountain and its slightly lower sister, Little Savage Mountain, were named after an early surveyor, John Savage. In 1755, during its expedition against the French, General Braddock's army experienced a misadventure descending one of the Savages and lost several wagons. (Courtesy of Frostburg State University Library.)

As local folks have always known, winters in western Maryland do not necessarily end with the beginning of spring. Cold weather and snow can continue well beyond the third week of March and are particularly unpredictable in the mountains. Hazardous road conditions require steady maintenance along the highways. Travel along the National Road in its early heyday often came to a halt during heavy snowfalls and continued to be difficult even as mechanized road-clearing machinery became available. In the above photograph, road crews have managed to clear a single lane of the pike atop Big Savage Mountain after a heavy snowfall at the end of April 1928. (Courtesy of Albert and Angela Feldstein.)

After descending Little Savage Mountain, travelers passed the farm once owned by Maryland's first governor, Thomas Johnson. Johnson purchased parcels from the State of Maryland, Revolutionary War soldiers (military lots), and others. While he never lived at the farm, he passed it on to family members when he died in 1819. It remained in the Johnson family until well into the 20th century. As can be seen in this photograph, the National Road passed between the Johnson home and farm buildings. (Courtesy of Virginia Williams Kelly.)

In 1806, in compliance with the legislation calling for the construction of the Cumberland Road, the three appointed commissioners sought to develop "the shortest road with the most benefits." Consequently, portions of the road were laid out in a manner that hewed to this directive despite the availability of easier routes with lower grades. Proponents of the Good Roads Movement sometimes cited a portion of road known as the "Long Stretch" as an example of this point. The Long Stretch is shown above and below from different perspectives. This segment of the pike ran in a virtual straight line for 2.5 miles between the base of Little Savage Mountain and the approach to Red Ridge, near the town of Piney Grove. (Both, courtesy of Virginia Williams Kelly.)

Heading west, the Long Stretch culminates in a section of road known as the "Shades of Death." This area was described by historians Karen Koegler and Kenneth Pavelchak as "a spooky enclave where the branches of towering pines hid robbers who preyed on National Road travelers." Over the years, the pines were largely cut down, as can be seen in this photograph of an auto approaching the Shades of Death (above). (Courtesy of Maryland State Archives, Leo Beachy Photographs.)

Nighttime robbery and theft of cargo were serious concerns. Thomas Searight recounted an incident involving stage drivers hired to transport US mail: "[T]heir calling through the dismal shades of death and other dark regions in the mountains with big, tempting mail bags in their charge no doubt turned their minds to what they considered a speedy, if not altogether a safe method of getting money." The miscreants fled to Canada but were returned to Maryland for trial. In the image at right, travelers are taking precautions against burglary. (Courtesy of *Harper's Monthly*, author's collection.)

Road conditions continued to be a source of concern in the first decade of the 1900s. An article in *Good Roads* magazine described the road between Frostburg and Grantsville in 1908 as "a little less rough than a creek bottom and hardly better for travel." The author pointed out that the area in eastern Garrett County "is farming country in which little money is available for road work, and conditions [in 1908] were about as unfavorable as they well could be to the making of extensive improvements." The situation in Allegany County was about the same until the middle of the second decade of the 1900s, when the state began to resurface portions of the western sector of the pike. The photograph above was taken six miles west of Frostburg before roadwork began. The photograph below graphically depicts the difficulties facing motorists on unimproved roadways on the pike. (Both, courtesy of Virginia Williams Kelly.)

After passing through the Shades of Death, travelers heading west crossed Red Ridge, where, during the heyday of the pike, two hotels were available to welcome them. According to Thomas Searight, a tavern about two miles farther west in tiny Piney Grove served as a regular stopping point for several stagecoach lines and was also popular with wagoners. Piney Grove sat 2,600 feet above sea level, in a valley between Red Ridge and Meadow Mountain. The automobile in this photograph is heading east toward Piney Grove (visible in the distance) after descending Meadow Mountain. (Courtesy of Virginia Williams Kelly.)

Repairing roads in the days before the widespread availability of mechanized equipment was slow, laborious, and exhausting. Maintenance and improvement of roadways was a county responsibility in the late 1800s and early 1900s. The crew in this photograph is working on the road approaching Grantsville from the east. (Courtesy of Virginia Williams Kelly.)

During the moribund period of the National Road in the second half of the 19th century, many of the once-crowded inns along the road closed their doors. In many cases, the buildings were repurposed or abandoned. When automobiles revived the pike, a need for hostelries arose. All-purpose rest stops appeared, and with them came something akin to motels. Clusters of cabins like those on Meadow Mountain in the above photograph began springing up to accommodate the increasing number of excursioners. (Courtesy of Albert and Angela Feldstein.)

Tomlinson's Inn was one of the oldest stops on the Cumberland Road. Jesse Tomlinson, who also owned a nearby inn called the Red House, recognized the commercial potential of the new road. In 1818, he built a large inn astride the road. Tomlinson owned a huge tract of land, inaugurated several other enterprises, and served for several years in the state legislature. J. Thomas Scharf, in his *History of Western Maryland*, reported that Tomlinson "in his day . . . was the most important and influential man in the upper part of Allegany." The building that housed the inn is now a private dwelling. (Courtesy of Virginia Williams Kelly.)

As noted earlier, the many stone arch bridges on the Cumberland Road were admired for their beauty, sturdy construction, and durability. The bridge over the Castleman River near Grantsville was built in 1813 to accommodate traffic on the new road. At the time it was constructed, it was the largest single-span stone bridge in the country. During construction, there was considerable doubt that the stonework would be strong enough to support the bridge once the surrounding scaffolding was removed. Local lore testifies that the contractor was so worried that the bridge would not hold up that he had his crew take away the supports the night before the grand opening to make sure that the structure would not collapse. As is evident in the above photograph, the bridge met the challenge admirably. It remained in service until 1933, when it was replaced by a concrete and steel span (below). (Above, courtesy of Albert and Angela Feldstein; below, courtesy of Maryland Department of Transportation.)

The Casselman Inn has been an exemplar on the National Road since 1842. It was built by Solomon Sterner, who used local, handmade brick in its construction. Jacob Brown, a 19th-century Cumberland native who often contributed articles to local newspapers, wrote admiringly of Sterner and his establishment: "In all those flush years [1842 until his death in 1852] he had more than his share of business. He was obliging, generous and industrious.... His table was always crowded with substantial and rich edibles." The inn drew many drovers, who herded their cattle into the large corral before partaking of the hospitality inside. After Sterner's death, the inn changed hands and was renamed several times. In its 175-plus years, the hostelry has been called the Sterner House, Drovers' Inn, Farmers' Hotel, and Dorsey Hotel. The above photograph dates to the late 1800s, and the image below was captured in the early 1900s. (Above, courtesy of David Guiney; below, courtesy of Albert and Angela Feldstein.)

Grantsville is a direct product of the National Road. Sixty years before the coming of the pike, General Braddock's army camped in an area called Little Crossings, near the later location of the Casselman Bridge. Families soon began settling in the vicinity, often along the enlarged pathway created by Braddock's engineers. In 1785, Danial Grant, a Baltimore hotel owner, purchased an 1,100-acre tract called Cornucopia. He increased his holdings and in 1796 moved to the area and established a town in the center of his Cornucopia property. Grantsville's location along Braddock's Road placed it on the prime trading and travel route over the Allegany Mountains. When the Cumberland Road reached the area in 1816, Grantsville found itself a half-mile south of the new highway. The solution to this was a short move north. The town thrived as a way-station and agricultural center in its new location. In the above photograph, the path of the National Road through the center of Grantsville can be seen. The image below provides a ground-level view of the road as it becomes Grantsville's Main Street. (Above, courtesy of Albert and Angela Feldstein; below, courtesy of Maryland State Archives, Leo Beachy Photographs.)

In 1837, a Pennsylvanian, Henry Fuller, moved to Grantsville and purchased a tavern called the Lehman House. He demolished the building in 1843 and constructed an inn, the Fuller House, which had 18 rooms and a stable capable of housing 40 horses. The hostelry changed hands numerous times and ultimately became the National Hotel (above, in 1909). It stood as the oldest building in Grantsville until it was demolished in 1984. The Victoria Hotel (below) was built in 1905 by Ambrose and Mary Bevans. The text on the back of the postcard noted that "this is one of the newer types of hotels, having come into existence after the old taverns and inns had been relegated to the past." When Mary died in 1912, Ambrose passed the business to their daughter and opened a grocery store in Grantsville. The building is now an apartment house. (Both, courtesy of Albert and Angela Feldstein.)

Many citizens of Grantsville came out on a cold February day to see a team of Eskimo dogs pass on the National Road through town on the way to Washington, DC. The *Cumberland Times* reported that the team was led by Eli A. Smith, a US mail carrier who wagered $10,000 that he could lead his dog team 5,500 miles to deliver a letter to Pres. Teddy Roosevelt. Smith left Nome on November 14, 1905, and expected to arrive in Washington 15 months later, on February 20, 1907. He and his dog team traveled on snow to Valdes, Alaska, where they boarded a ship to Seattle and then mushed across the United States. Their sledge was equipped with wheels so that they could proceed without snow when necessary. The photograph below provides an idea of the condition of the pike in town after the weather has taken its toll on the roadbed. Both date to the first decade of the 1900s. (Above, courtesy of Albert and Angela Feldstein; below, courtesy of Maryland State Archives, Leo Beachy Photographs.)

During the palmy days of the National Pike, taverns dotted its landscape. A tavern near Grantsville, built in about 1820, was one of the oldest and well-known in the region. In 1832, the building became the Little Crossings Inn. It later became the Dixie Tavern (above) and then the Arlington. In a 1926 newspaper article, the 82-year-old daughter of a Dixie's proprietor recounted some of the lore passed down to her by her parents. She noted that the Dixie played host to prominent guests, including Andrew Jackson, Mexican general Santa Ana, Gen. Zachary Taylor (soon to become president of the United States), and a high-level party of Native Americans on the way to Washington to meet with "The Great White Father." It was believed that the Native American delegation was led by the famous Chief Blackhawk. (Courtesy of Albert and Angela Feldstein.)

Heading west from Grantsville, travelers passed over another of the sturdy stone bridges constructed expressly for the new Cumberland Road. The structure passed over Shade Run, near one of the camping areas for General Braddock's army on its way to Fort Duquesne in 1755. (Courtesy of Maryland State Roads Commission, Enoch Pratt Free Library.)

While easing and accelerating the process of building and repairing roads, mechanization did not eliminate the need for hard manual labor. This road crew in the 1910s is taking a break from smoothing the National Road near Grantsville. They also appear to be posturing for the camera! (Courtesy of Maryland State Archives, Leo Beachy Photographs.)

Improved roads did not guarantee trouble-free journeys. Tubeless tires did not become available until the 1940s, and replacing tires in the early 1900s was an expensive proposition. The men in this photograph are dealing with a blowout on the National Pike in western Maryland. (Courtesy of Maryland State Archives, Leo Beachy Photographs.)

There are several versions of the story behind the name Negro Mountain. Most, however, share a common thread involving Thomas Cresap, the pioneer who is credited, along with Native American guide Namacolin, with cutting the path that was the precursor to Braddock's Road and the National Road. Cresap had a large and imposing African American servant named Nemesis who accompanied him on an operation against local Native Americans. Nemesis had a premonition that he would die on this mission. Cresap offered to leave him behind, but Nemesis insisted on remaining with the party. His presentiment came true, and he was killed in the fight. The name *Negro Mountain* was a means of paying homage to this brave man. In recent times, attempts have been made to address possible sensitivities by changing the name. Opponents, including a prominent local African American woman, prevailed, and the name was retained. In modern times, the peak of the 2,900-foot mountain has housed commercial enterprises (above) and a fire tower (left). (Both, courtesy of Albert and Angela Feldstein.)

In the early days of automobile travel, cars often overheated while climbing to the summit of 2,900-foot Negro Mountain, the highest peak on the eastern portion of the National Road. The descent presented a different set of potential hazards. In the above photograph, journeyers are warned of a 1.75-mile descent and advised to "snub" (tap) the car's brakes rather than keeping constant foot pressure on them. The later sign (below) indicates that road work has reduced the length of the downward grade to one mile. In a nod to improvements in automobile technology, both signs tell drivers to put the cars in second gear to help slow down and apply their brakes only to snub to safe speeds. (Above, courtesy of Albert and Angela Feldstein; below, courtesy of David Guiney.)

From its inception, an important function of the National Road was to facilitate the transporting of mail. In an 1832 speech to Congress, Pennsylvania representative T.M.T. McKennan noted that, prior to the inception of the National Pike, "eight or more days were occupied in transporting the mail from Baltimore to Wheeling." With the completion of the pike, mail "is carried in comfortable stages, protected from the inclemency of the weather, in forty-eight hours." After delivery to the towns, however, the mail went no farther. Patrons had to travel to the post office to pick up their letters or parcels. This was particularly burdensome to farmers and others who lived miles from the nearest post office. In 1896, Rural Free Delivery was inaugurated on an experimental basis in three West Virginia towns. The service worked well, and by 1903, most of western Maryland was receiving free postal delivery service. The National Pike continued to be a major mail conduit. It was also used by local mail carriers. Most traveled in horse-drawn vehicles and, later, motorized conveyances. However, bicycles were another option. The mail carrier in this photograph is laboring up Negro Mountain to carry out his duties. (Courtesy of the Maryland Department, Enoch Pratt Free Library/Maryland's State Library Resource Center.)

The descent of Negro Mountain on the original National Road ended with a series of twists and turns leading to a stone bridge over Puzzley Run (above). (Several creeks in western Maryland and elsewhere are called "runs.") The bridge was designed to be "construction friendly." The road was laid out to reach the bridge at a 90-degree angle to permit the overpass to be as straight as possible. This was an efficient and cost-saving method utilized commonly at the time. It often resulted, however, in sharp turns in the road near each end of the bridge. This was not an insurmountable problem during the days of slow-moving vehicles on the National Road. However, the advent of fast-moving automobiles in the 20th century presented serious hazards to motorists. Consequently, in the case of the Puzzley Run bridge, the road was realigned in 1932 to lessen the angle of the curve (below). The old bridge was bypassed and today sits on private property. (Above, courtesy of Western Maryland Historical Library; below, courtesy of Maryland State Highway Administration and the Maryland Department, Enoch Pratt Free Library/Maryland's State Library Resource Center.)

The pike on the western slope of Negro Mountain dips into a hollow before crossing Puzzley Run and heading up the final slope before entering Pennsylvania. In this photograph, the auto is nearing the downgrade. Keysers Ridge can be seen in the distance. (Courtesy of Virginia Williams Kelly.)

This photograph, taken in 1884, provides a close view of the Puzzley Run bridge and the final curve on the western slope of Negro Mountain. A traveler describing the descent 35 years later made clear that little had changed in the challenge and the rewards: "We came down this mountain 2,908 feet above sea level—most of the way on low. Some drive I'll say—We are sure seeing some beautiful scenery." (Courtesy of Maryland State Archives, Leo Beachy Photographs.)

Keysers Ridge was the final peak before exiting Maryland's portion of the National Road and entering Pennsylvania. At 2,800 feet in elevation, it was only slightly lower than its neighbor, Negro Mountain. Writing about his 1915 trip, Robert Bruce noted that "in the olden days this section [of the National Road] was 'snowed up' oftener than any other stretch on the road, sometimes to a depth of twenty feet, stopping stage coaches and freight wagons for days at a time." This photograph suggests that things had not changed very much in the early 20th century. (Courtesy of Albert and Angela Feldstein.)

The original purpose of the National Road was to provide a unifying linkage between America's east and its new western territories. In 1931, a chapter of the Daughters of the American Revolution erected a monument memorializing "The pioneers who with heroic sacrifice and undaunted courage blazed this old trail now known as the National Highway and thus opened 'The Gateway to the West.'" (Courtesy of the Maryland Department, Enoch Pratt Free Library/Maryland's State Library Resource Center.)

The National Road crosses the Mason-Dixon Line from Maryland into Pennsylvania three miles northwest of Keysers Ridge. After 1835, when Pennsylvania assumed control of its portion of the pike, travelers venturing two miles into Pennsylvania encountered the Keystone State's Tollhouse No. 1 in what is today the town of Addison. In the photograph above, taken from the Maryland line into Pennsylvania, the mile marker informs journeyers that Wheeling is 96 miles away and Petersburg is two miles up the road. (Petersburg was renamed Addison in 1832.) The reverse scene is captured in the photograph below. The photographer was standing in Pennsylvania and pointing his camera toward Maryland. The mile marker seen in the above image is visible on the left, behind the auto. (Both, courtesy of Western Maryland Historical Library.)

As noted earlier, the National Road has had many names during its over-200-year history. In 1926, the practice of naming roads with words was replaced by a nationwide numerical system. State roads not assigned a national numerical designation were ascribed numbers by state or local authorities. Much of the old National Road was labeled US Route 40. In ensuing years, as newer roads and then interstates were constructed, the old road was often bypassed and assigned state or county numbers. Today, portions of the road in Maryland remain US 40. Other portions are called Alternate US 40 (US 40A), Maryland Route 144, Scenic US 40, Interstate 70, and Interstate 68. The early word names, however, have not been completely eliminated. The entire stretch of road, incorporating all the numerical designations, is often referred to as the National Road, National Highway, Historic National Road, and other appellations. Individual sections carry monikers such as Old National Pike, Baltimore National Pike, National Freeway, and others in addition to their assigned numbers. (Courtesy of Babs Savitt.)

Visit us at
arcadiapublishing.com

www.ingramcontent.com/pod-product-compliance
Lightning Source LLC
Chambersburg PA
CBHW060923170426
43191CB00025B/2462